Ginny

GINNY
An Autobiography

VIRGINIA LENG
with Genevieve Murphy

A Methuen Paperback

First published in Great Britain 1986
by Stanley Paul & Co Ltd
This paperback edition first published 1987
by Methuen London Ltd, 11 New Fetter Lane, London EC4P 4EE
© 1986, 1987 Virginia Leng

Printed in Great Britain by
Richard Clay Ltd, Bungay, Suffolk

British Library Cataloguing in Publication Data

Leng, Virginia
    Ginny : an autobiography.
    1. Leng, Virginia   2. Show jumpers (Persons)
    — Great Britain — Biography
    I. Title   II. Murphy, Genevieve
    798.2′4′0924   SF295.5

    ISBN 0 – 413 – 14930 – 7

To my mother, Uncle Jack,
Dot and the boys

Contents

List of Illustrations

ONE
Around the world

By all accounts I was a bit of a monster during the first few years of my life. Since I can remember nothing about it, I have to assume that the stories told about me are nothing but the truth.

'You weren't too bad as a baby,' says my mother. There is a reflective pause while she remembers the fat and ugly infant in the pram, before she adds, 'Though, of course, you looked more like a prize boxer than a baby.'

I was the second of her two children, born on 1 February 1955 in Malta, where my father was then serving with the Royal Marines. Everyone loved my brother, Michael, who is four years older than me, but I was impossible.

I screamed all through my christening and on enough occasions after it to make the maid my parents had in Malta pack her bags and leave. 'And I didn't blame her,' says my mother. Apparently, I wasn't '*too* bad' during some of the short time I lived in Malta, nor during another brief period in Cyprus before my parents moved to Canada. By the time we reached Canadian soil I had learned to move and that, I am told, is when I became a real nightmare.

My mother's friends refused to go shopping with her if I were to be in tow. By then I had acquired the art of disappearing, swiftly and silently, as soon as Mummy took her eyes off me. Afterwards I was usually to be found causing extreme embarrassment in the men's changing rooms at the huge supermarket in Kingston, which is on the east end of Lake Ontario. On one occasion I chose a different route and ended up in a display window, among the sleek and elegantly dressed wax figures, wearing a large hat that I had nicked from one of them and glaring out at the passing shoppers.

And if these little escapades weren't enough, I also managed to disappear over the side of a yacht into the depths of Lake Ontario. Needless to say, my mother can recall this incident fairly vividly: 'We were living outside Kingston at the Canadian Army Staff College and

11

had made great friends with a British couple, Peter and Jackie Wilson, who were also stationed there. Peter was a keen sailor and on that particular day we'd been mucking about in his yacht intending to go sailing. At some stage we heard a plop and thought that a spanner had been dropped overboard, then suddenly this thing appeared gulping and with eyes out on stalks and I yelped, "It's not a spanner, it's Virginia!" '

Apparently I owe my life to Peter Wilson, who promptly dived into the lake and fished me out. It would be nice to think that this experience did something to curb my instinct for disappearing, but I'm afraid my mother is unable to recall the slightest sign of improvement in my behaviour.

I was three when I first saw England. My father had been given a new post at the Ministry of Defence in London. So we spent a few years in Kent, living in the first-floor flat of a large building ('a big old monstrosity' according to my mother) which belonged to the Ministry. Mummy wasted no time in booking riding lessons for me at a place near Ightham. By her standards, I was starting a little late at the age of three. She had been riding when she was only two and had her first fall when she was so small that she was pulled off by a bramble.

I went to the riding school once a week and rode a tiny Shetland pony, until my mother bought a Welsh Mountain mare called Misty through a newspaper advert. Misty was then living seven miles away from us, so Mummy and two of her friends organised a rota system to walk the little mare to her new home. My mother was reminded of the journey at the 1985 Bath and West Show, when she ran into one of the people who had been on that rota about 25 years earlier. 'It's somewhat different from walking Misty home through the Kent lanes at some unearthly hour of the night,' said the lady who had done her two-mile stint.

Michael went away to prep school while we were in Kent, and I became a pupil at Mrs Kitney's kindergarten school in a little village called Stanstead. Like most of the others I regarded the moment that my mother came to take me home as the best time of the day. In my case it really was rather special, because Mummy arrived on her show hack called Golden Melody, with Misty alongside on a leading-rein. No doubt I was very cocky in front of my school mates as I left the classroom to clamber on my pony and ride home.

I was jumping – albeit tiny cavalletti – at the age of three and hunting on a leading-rein when I was four. 'I didn't take you over any vast jumps,' says my mother, 'but you managed all the little ones.' I seem to remember screeching, 'I can't do it' and finding myself at the other side while I was still protesting.

Misty knew exactly how to cope with me. Riding her in the field at the age of four or five, I tended to keep booting her on, wanting to go faster. She would put up with me quite happily until she'd had enough. She would then jog trot calmly across the field, with me pulling and yanking to no avail, until she reached the ditch on the far side. Once there, she would stop and drop her shoulder, dumping me neatly into the ditch.

My pony was probably glad to see the back of me when, at the age of six, I went by troop ship with my mother to join my father in Singapore. Michael stayed behind at boarding school, and Misty went to a quieter home in Kent with Uncle Jack (my mother's brother, Major Jack Rice) where she had a foal whom we called Dandy Kim.

In Singapore I met Vivien Eggar and the two of us (known as 'the terrible twins') became inseparable. Our favourite pastime was eating. We both shared the same insatiable appetite for boiled eggs and toast soldiers, washed down by as many chocolate milk shakes as we could lay our hands on. We would probably have looked like barn doors if we hadn't spent so much time galloping around on our broomstick hobby horses, whose heads were made from socks. We loved them so much that we took them with us into the swimming pool, which must have looked ridiculous.

I was the one who felt ridiculous on the day when Vivien and I were both bridesmaids, wearing long dresses with very full waist slips underneath. I was half way up the aisle, doing my best to look suitably demure in this totally unaccustomed feminine outfit, when I suddenly had difficulty in walking. 'Slow down,' I hissed at Vivien. Not understanding my predicament, she signalled at me to stay quiet and continued walking at the same pace.

By now the waist slip, which I had failed to secure properly, was appearing at my feet. I looked down in horror as yard after yard of white material spread around me on the floor entangling my feet so that I was forced to stop. 'Step out of it,' said a lady beside me in the aisle seat.

Everyone in the church, either hearing her voice or wondering what had become of the other bridesmaid, turned round to look at me. In an agony of embarrassment I stumbled out of the slip, and the lady at my side put it into her capacious handbag. When I rejoined Vivien it must have been very noticeable that the skirt of one bridesmaid's dress was hanging in full and elegant folds while the other's was limp and straight!

I felt far more comfortable in the tomboy clothes I wore when Vivien and I (plus the hobby horses) went with parents and friends for our regular Sunday picnics on the Two Sisters Islands – where we had to keep a sharp look out for dangerous snakes, both on land and in the water. When we were returning from one of these picnics, I saw a kitten being thrown into the sea at Singapore docks and went rushing off to rescue it, while my mother screamed at me to come back.

The kitten was half dead by the time I grabbed it out of the sea and we took it home, back to the saintly amah who had the impossible task of looking after me, but it survived. We called him Tiger Royal, and he grew into the most amazing cat. He could take a running leap up the wall, catch one of the tiny lizards that had come to sit on our ceiling and then do a backward flip to land on all four feet.

I went to the Tanglin School in Singapore with Vivien (whose father, Brigadier Eggar and his wife, Ann, have since done a tremendous amount of work for horse trials in Britain, helping as timekeepers and so on). By then I was quite a tomboy. I'd played rough-and-tumble games with my brother and couldn't have cared less about all the more ladylike pastimes.

My mother was appalled by my behaviour when I had a major fight with the big bully of the school. I told him to push off, because we'd all had enough of him. He retaliated by throwing me against a pillar and smashing my two front teeth. Wild with fury that gave me amazing strength, I pinned the bully to the floor and spat on him, while people stood watching, completely mesmerised. I tried to play down my own part in all this when I returned home with two teeth missing but, needless to say, the headmistress gave a full account to my horrified mother!

This unladylike brawl chipped one of my adult teeth, as we discovered when it emerged with a corner missing, and it later had to be crowned. I probably looked like Dracula by the time I had my first kiss. I was about seven and the wonderful Christopher Graham-Hogg was a few years older. I had pursued him with wings on my feet during our games of kiss-chase, in which the person who was 'it' chased whoever they wanted to kiss the most. Then, one unforgettable day, I went into a huge monsoon drain with Christopher and he gave me a thrilling peck on the cheek – my first kiss! I felt terribly adult.

I think my parents were also enjoying the Singapore experience. My mother and her new friend, Moysie Barton, were making the most of the wonderful opportunity to ride in flat races. Moysie and her husband, Robert, who now live within a few miles of us, have remained close friends. Meanwhile my father, who was a Commando in the Royal Marines, did some long treks through the jungle. Returning from one of these journeys, he told us about the instructions he always gave to his subalterns: 'There's one essential thing to remember. When you get up in the morning, for goodness sake shake out your boots because that's the favourite hiding place for scorpions.'

On that occasion, one of the chaps (who was not the brightest boy in the world) had got up and, remembering the instruction, had carefully shaken out his boots. Sure enough, a scorpion fell out, so he promptly trod on it with his bare foot to kill it. The lad was unharmed, but my father couldn't believe that anyone could have been so stupid. Another time out in the jungle, my father told me, he had cut himself very badly and had to sew himself together with needle and thread. It was a result of stories like these that he became my great hero.

Another of the lasting friendships made in Singapore was with Pat Baker, though it didn't get off to a very good start. Pat, then in his early twenties, was working at the polo club and my mother went there to ask him whether I could ride one of the ponies. Because I was only six at the time, he said it was out of the question. Never one to take no for an answer without resistance, my mother told him that age should have nothing to do with it, all that mattered was whether I had the ability.

'There really was no answer to that,' she tells me. 'I think he wondered what he'd done to deserve this terrible woman and her spoilt brat. He was wonderful with all the older children who went there to ride, but he didn't think a child of your age would be able to cope. So he put you up on the worst pony he could find and it bucked like mad, but you stayed on – which was rather gratifying for me. After that, he couldn't really refuse to take you.'

Apart from sorting out a polo pony for her 'spoilt brat' to ride, my mother helped to run the Singapore branch of the Pony Club and it was flourishing by the time we once again packed our bags and sailed home to England. I was by then an uninhibited seven-year-old and the age of 'the twist' had just started. I had been taught this fashionable new dance by Digby Willoughby (who is now in charge of the Cresta Run in St Moritz) when he came out to Singapore. Two of us – Nick Sturge, who was serving in the Royal Dragoon Guards, and myself – then taught the twist to virtually everyone on board the ship that brought us home.

It was about that time that we began taking an annual family ski-ing holiday in Switzerland. I was an absolute lunatic on skis and loved every moment – except the queueing. I remember standing in a queue with Michael (feeling very important because I was ski-ing with my big brother, who had reached the mature age of eleven by then) when a Frenchman zipped down the slopes and pushed into the line between Michael and myself.

'What do you mean by queue-barging,' said my brother, growing to his full 5 feet 2 inches. 'This is my sister and we've been standing here for about an hour.'

The Frenchman, aged about 22, completely ignored us. So I took a few steps back and prodded him in the rump with my ski-stick. He turned on Michael and said, '*Who* do you think you are?'

'I'm Cassius Clay and she's Brigitte Bardot,' came the retort, which seemed positively brilliant to me. The chap then went to the end of the queue.

We were reminded of those ski-ing holidays towards the end of 1985, when my mother had a surprise telephone call. 'This is Norbert from Switzerland,' came the voice at the other end. 'You haven't forgotten me?'

We certainly had not forgotten, though it was many years since we had last seen or heard from him. Norbert, then a university student, had been my ski-ing instructor some four years running when we stayed in a tiny Swiss village completely off the beaten track. He had visited us for a few days when we were in Devon and still had our old telephone number; it had taken him about half an hour to get the new one, but he was determined to make contact. 'How is Ginny?' Norbert wanted to know. Apparently he had seen me on television in Switzerland and, on that reckoning, had the mistaken idea that I must be famous!

We had gone to live in Devon on our return from Singapore, first in a thatched cottage and later in a house my parents bought near Silverton. Misty and Dandy Kim came to join us. Michael was there in the school holidays and my father, now back with the Ministry of Defence in London, came home at weekends. Then I was sent off to become a weekly boarder at the Convent of the Assumption at Sidmouth and began longing for the weekends when I, too, could go home.

I *hated* school. I was always crying for my mother, and every Sunday I tried to make myself ill so that I wouldn't have to go back on

16

Monday. I suppose that the school wasn't too bad and the poor nuns must have found me a nightmare. If I wasn't crying, I was accepting some ridiculous dare that was to land me in trouble. The reason why the school seemed so ghastly was because I hated being away from home.

It was during that time that my mother first met our vet, Don Attenburrow. She had called him out to look at one of the ponies. 'I knocked on the door of a thatched cottage,' says Don, 'and I came face to face with a very smart young lady. We both eyed each other with grave suspicion.'

My smart young mother was later to take a keen interest in Don's research into respiratory problems in horses, through which he became a Fellow of the Royal College of Veterinary Surgeons. His research has always been done through general practice; he has always believed in 'non-invasive' experimentation, preferring to study the horses that came to him with problems rather than abuse a fit horse by deliberately causing the condition which would aid his research. My mother helped him by occasionally testing his new equipment.

I was seven when Don and my mother first met. It can't have been long afterwards when, during breakfast time at school, a mistress came in and said, 'I'd like to have a word with you, Virginia.' She took me outside and told me that our house had been burnt to the ground and that my mother was coming to take me out to tea. The fact that the thatched cottage had gone up in flames seemed unimportant compared with the marvellous news that I was to be taken out for tea.

Apparently all the others had been told not to stare at me, because there had been a great disaster in my life. But they were normal, inquisitive girls and all eyes were on me as I returned to the dining room. It made me feel terribly important. My mother came with strawberries and we went on to the beach at Sidmouth to enjoy this special treat. What does a house matter, I thought, when you can sit on a beach and feast yourself on strawberries?

My mother's story is not quite as cheerful. 'It was on 14 June and very cold for that time of year, so cold that I lit the fire. It had been lit many times before but on that occasion something caught fire in the chimney – and that was it. The thatch was about 3 feet thick and, once it started burning, there wasn't much you could do to stop it – water just tended to beat the flames back in. The whole of the top floor went and it was a horrible experience. I can remember standing, with water dripping everywhere, and thinking that I hadn't even a toothbrush to my name. Then the telephone rang and someone invited me to dinner. I felt very foolish replying, ''No I can't come out to dinner because the house is on fire.'' '

For the best part of a year after the fire our family home was a large caravan, which had a sitting room, two bedrooms and an outside loo. My parents had bought a lovely old house called Ford, near Silverton, which actually appeared in the Domesday Book. It was then split into two houses and hadn't been lived in for donkey's years, so we used the caravan until the house was habitable. My mother did much of the restoration and decoration herself. She would occasionally decide that we needed to bash down a wall and, looking back, it was probably lucky that the whole building didn't collapse!

After we had moved into the house, my mother did wonderful work on the garden, creating lawns and flower beds out of a jungle. She was alone in the house one night when she heard the ominous sound of crunching on the gravel outside and, thinking burglars had arrived, she grabbed the poker, switched on the outside light and opened the front door. There she came face to face with about ten bullocks, who were happily trampling round her beautiful garden.

There was nothing she could do about it that night, and when she woke the following morning they were still there. Daylight revealed the trampled lawns and flower beds. In fury, my mother phoned Farmer Cole, who lived up the road. 'Would you please get down here *immediately*,' she said. 'Your bullocks have virtually ruined my garden.'

He sauntered down about two hours later, put his hat on the back of his head and listened to my mother's tirade. 'What are you going to do about it?' she asked. 'Just look at the mess; your ten bullocks have done all this damage.'

'Well, my dear,' he said, 'you were lucky it wasn't twenty.'

With that, he rounded up his bullocks and took them back up the road, leaving my mother (for once) without an answer. The farmer's logic was irrefutable!

We were to discover that Farmer Cole actually bred The Poacher, the marvellous horse with whom Ben Jones won an Olympic team gold medal in 1968 and Richard Meade won Badminton in 1970. The farmer had no idea about his claim to fame until we told him. Richard had said he was sure that The Poacher's breeder lived somewhere near us and we managed to trace the horse's previous life back to the place where he was foaled.

We had been in Devon almost five years when my father was given a new post as Military Attaché in the Philippines. It was decided that I should be taken away from the school I still loathed and go with my parents to Manila, while Michael continued his studies at Haileybury.

Preparations to go abroad were even more complicated than usual. There were ponies to be sold (including Misty and Dandy Kim); the house and its 30 acres of land were to be let, and my mother had to find someone to look after her two horses (Tia Maria and Benedictine) until we returned. Rosemary Thomas, a friend who lived nearby, agreed to take care of the horses, with Don Attenburrow to help with veterinary advice. Our main problem seemed to be solved.

Then one day, a few weeks before our departure, my mother and I looked in horror as a lorry came to a crunching halt on our gravel drive. Behind, in a Sunbeam sports car, was the unmistakable aristocratic figure of Ewart Rice, my grandpa. It could mean only one thing: grandpa had indulged his passion for buying horses.

'Oh Lord, not again,' said my mother. She had seen her father turn up behind a lorry on previous occasions and usually about a dozen miserable specimens, bought in one of the Devon or Cornwall markets, would be dumped on us.

'I thought they needed a good home,' Grandpa would say, as though he were being perfectly reasonable. My mother would then have to break, school and sell them, hoping to get rid of one lot before the next arrived. I have to admit that I enjoyed my grandfather's addiction.

On the day I have mentioned, when our departure for the Philippines was imminent, my mother and I had been moving the remainder of Grandpa's last purchase from the lower field to the orchard. Even I could see that we didn't need any more. When the ramp was let down we found there was just one poor little colt, looking very frightened and lost. He was a six-month-old sucker, bought by my grandfather for £35 at Five Lanes Cattle Market.

'What on earth did you want to buy *that* for,' asked my mother, exasperated. 'It won't make 15·2 hh unless it's very lucky.'

Grandpa, who loved to barter and was never happier than when he felt he had bought a bargain, was not in the best of tempers. A sour note had crept in when he had been forced to part with an extra £12 in order to get the colt delivered to us and, having gone to this additional expense, he reckoned that my mother should at least be grateful.

'Just wait and see,' he said, stiffly, after my mother's disparaging remarks. 'Anyway, he's for Virginia.'

Whether he made 15·2 hh or not, I would have my very own horse to replace the ponies who were leaving us. So I let Mummy and Grandpa argue between themselves. I wasn't fussed!

We called the colt Dubonnet. At that stage my mother called all the horses after drinks and I was happy with the name, which I swiftly shortened to Dubby. Rosemary Thomas came up trumps again by agreeing to accommodate the newcomer, as well as the other two horses, while we were away in Manila.

I was about twelve when my parents and I embarked on the ship that was to take us on our three-week journey to the Philippines. Inevitably, the excitement of being on board began to wear a little thin after the first thrilling days at sea and I made the most of all the things that were there to keep us occupied − deck hockey, swimming, gymnastics and so on.

When we reached Bombay, I decided that I didn't much fancy being dragged round to see the sights. So my parents went off together, leaving me on the ship. I was aimlessly drifting around when I saw some children begging on the docks. It was a sight that pulled the heartstrings and demanded instant action.

I crept stealthily into the ship's kitchen, stole a batch of loaves and a basket, then found a rope, which I used to lower the bread to the hungry children below. They received my offering like manna from heaven. As I remember it, the process of stealing loaves and lowering them to the gathering crowd of grateful children went on for about an hour, until I was caught red-handed − by which time it seemed as though half the population of Bombay had gathered in earnest on the docks! I was then told that I had been very, very naughty and must never think of doing such a thing again. But I was still thrilled with my afternoon's work.

I was to start a new school when we reached Manila and it proved to be another rather miserable experience, though at least it was a day school and I could escape from it each afternoon. I was the only fair-haired, English-speaking, Church of England pupil. The rest of the schoolgirls were dark-haired, Catholic Filipinos, who spoke Tagalog. I did not enjoy feeling almost like an imposter, because I was so totally different.

Sport is supposed to build bridges between nations, but my attempt to teach football to the Filipino schoolgirls was not a roaring success. I booted a football straight through the window of the Reverend Mother's office − and we stuck to volley ball, the normal sport of the school, after that. Outside school the girls never ventured forth without a chaperone. The fact that I was allowed to walk up to the

Polo Club on my own to have a swim was considered very shocking. There was such a wide difference in our upbringing that it was bound to be hard for me to fit in.

The Polo Club in the Philippines is probably the finest in the world, with a very smart social side as well as opportunities to ride and swim. We lived about ten minutes' walk away and had many wonderful times there. We went as guest members, which meant that we were not allowed to hire the riding school horses belonging to the club, but that was no hardship since two of the polo players – Colonel Jake Zobel (a very important man in the Philippines) and Chito Cacho – allowed us to ride their ponies.

The Pony Club was also based there, run by my mother and her great friend Jenny Malcolm, who now lives in Australia. They did a tremendous amount of work, organising things like moonlight rides, breakfast rides and gymkhanas, generally getting the Pony Club on the right road. It has grown ever since, as I discovered when I went back there to teach in 1980 – but that later visit belongs to another part of my story.

Though I didn't know it at the time, my father was then suffering from multiple sclerosis. He had always led an active life and might have played rugger for England if he hadn't been living in a caravan somewhere on the British coast when the selectors issued their invitation. I wasn't born then, but my mother remembers it well. 'He'd played rugger for the Royal Navy and for Edinburgh Wanderers in Scotland, in fact he was invited to play in a Scottish final trial but turned it down because it meant that he couldn't then be picked for England. He'd also played for Blackheath and against the All Blacks, so was hoping that the call would come to play for England. But unfortunately, when it did, it never reached him. His job at the time was measuring the depth of the sea around the coastline, which meant that we lived in a caravan and moved on every two or three weeks. The selectors left a telephone message somewhere, telling him to be in a certain place on a given date for the final trial, but it didn't get to him.'

Apart from playing rugger and trekking through the jungle, my father held the Royal Navy records for pole vault and long jump. Though he rode and hunted, horses were never a major part of his active life, which was slowly ending as the multiple sclerosis took hold. He was a great success as an attaché in Manila, and everyone adored him. He had great charm and was very good looking, which meant that he was constantly surrounded by women. He lapped up

21

their attention.

While we were in the Philippines, I gradually became aware that he was becoming less active, less ready to join in all the things that we had enjoyed doing together. But I had no idea that the disease which was slowly paralysing him had already been diagnosed.

TWO
Back home to school

I was thirteen when I became a boarder at Bedgebury Park in Kent. My name had been down for Benenden, a much more famous Kent school, but I wasn't up to the academic level required! My mother says that, with all the moving, I didn't really have a chance to come up to Benenden scratch. I'm pleased that she has given me a plausible excuse.

'When I went to see Bedgebury, I liked it so much that I thought it was probably nicer,' says my mother. 'You had plenty of variety and many different nationalities which, to me, is terribly important. I thought it was super.'

It didn't seem that 'super' to me. My mother delivered me there before flying back to join my father in the Philippines, leaving me with another chronic dose of homesickness. Uncle Jack lived nearby and he helped me to survive the years at boarding school by collecting me and my friends for the Easter holidays and the odd weekend. Feeding us seemed like an endless task because we all seemed like hollow trees. He still recounts the day he tried to over-face us with a vast steak and a mountain of meringue and strawberries – but we scoffed the lot.

I flew out to Manila twice a year, for the Christmas and summer holidays, usually on my own. I was normally delivered to the airport by Uncle Jack and, of course, collected by my mother at the other end. But it was a very long journey, with several changes of crew en route, and I felt very adult making it alone. I can remember, at the age of thirteen, doing myself up to look the part of the sophisticated traveller with a little lipstick and make-up to disguise the third-form schoolgirl look. On the plane I chatted in a very grown-up way (or so I thought) to the man sitting next to me and then got cold feet because I had become uncomfortably aware that he was showing rather too much interest in me. He must have seen a crack appear in the thin layer of sophistication which I had put on with the lipstick, because he suddenly asked me my age. I looked at him with innocent eyes and answered, 'Thirteen.'

There was a horrified pause before he said, 'Oh Lord, I suppose we'd better have a game of Battleships.'

I stopped off in Singapore on that journey to the Philippines. M father had given me a beautiful Tissot watch for my thirteenth birthday, which was my pride and joy; I couldn't stop looking at m wris: while I was wearing it. For some idiotic reason, I decided that wouldn't wear it during dinner at the hotel in Singapore because might lose it. So I left it hidden in my room and, when I went bac there after the meal, it had vanished. I was distraught by the theft o my lovely watch, and my parents were later furious with me fo being so stupid as to leave it in the hotel bedroom.

Probably the most embarrassing moment of my entire life occurre during one of those trips to Manila in my early teens. We stopped i Hong Kong, where I went swimming in the new bikini which I ha saved up for and bought with great pride. I thought I looke stunning in it, the best thing since Brigitte Bardot. Having leapt int the swimming pool, I then came out and realised it was see-through I was mortified that my bust, which resembled two little hazel nuts should have been on public display. In the agony of embarrassmen that followed, I refused even to go out and sit in the sun, let alon accept the offer to borrow a non-see-through bathing costume an go back in the swimming pool.

Apart from the problems with the watch and the bikini, my trips t Manila were wonderful. Michael, whose holidays were usually o slightly different dates from mine, also flew out on his own and w had a great family reunion. It was always a wrench to leave m parents and get on the plane that was to take me back to boardin school at Bedgebury Park.

There are now marvellous riding facilities at my old school but while I was there, anyone keen on horses had to go to Benenden where Princess Anne was by then in the sixth form. I can remembe seeing her on a chestnut horse called Oporto, while I was riding scruffy little dun four-year-old who looked like an urchin. The Princess and I shared the same instructor Cherry Hatton-Hall, but the difference in our ages meant that w were never on the same ride.

I tended to be put on the bucking broncos, which would have bee good fun except that we seemed to ride round and round in circle for ever, while I was itching to jump. I put up with the endless circle in the hope that we would eventually leave the floor and take of over fences – and I did get a little jumping, though not nearly enough to suit my book. I also took part in the Benenden quadrille, which I thoroughly enjoyed.

I loved acting in the school plays and put far more effort into them than into the academic subjects I was supposed to be learning. My favourite role was as an old schoolmistress. I can't remember the name of the play, but I recall being kitted out in grey wig and bun, round spectacles, voluminous tweed suit, woollen stockings and brogues. I also used to play the guitar – and belt out the accompanying songs – with a friend called Caroline Taylor. Needless to say, our voices were not quite in harmony and we were banished to the changing rooms to practise becoming the next Simon and Garfunkel!

It has to be admitted that I behaved very badly at Bedgebury Park. I was once dared to hide on top of a bookcase in the library while the teachers were having their dinner, so that I would be able to tape record their entire conversation. The dinner seemed to last for ever and my hiding place became more and more uncomfortable, before the teachers eventually cleared out and the girls – among them my best friend, Paris Hutton – rushed in to help me down from the bookcase. They arrived in the nick of time. I had only just clambered down when a mistress walked in and we had to hide the tape recorder swiftly.

'Where have you been?' she asked me, severely. 'You were not at supper, were you?'

I promptly burst into tears and told a white lie: 'I was hiding because I was homesick.' In fact, the excitement of accepting the dare had briefly overcome my normally continual state of longing to be with my parents.

I found myself lunching in the same library in 1985, when I went back to Bedgebury Park to open the new indoor riding school. I felt very brave recounting the story of how I had hidden on the bookcase, but they all roared with laughter. Incidentally, the tape recording was a dead loss. None of the teachers talked about any of the schoolgirls and the whole point of the exercise was to hear their views on us.

While I was a pupil at Bedgebury, I had anorexia nervosa. Jessica, one of my friends, had suggested she and I should go on a diet because she reckoned we were both too fat. She eventually stopped dieting, but I carried on until it became an obsession. I still loved food – that was part of the obsession. I would have been happy if I could have spent hours preparing a delicious meal, but, ironically, I would have wanted to watch someone else eat it. I cheated when they weighed me by putting stones in my pockets. I had a bag under the table during meal times, so that I could put food into it and pretend I'd eaten. If I did eat more than a few scraps, I deliberately made myself sick afterwards.

I was down to 6 stone 3 pounds when my mother flew home from the Philippines to see me and, although I thought my skinny figure looking stunning, she must have had an awful shock. She handled it marvellously. There is no way you can insist that a true anorexia case – which I believe I was – must eat. The condition is entirely psychological and my mother hit on the one and only thing that was likely to sway me. She said that I needed my strength if I were to be any good at riding and all the other sports I loved, that I needed to eat in order to have sufficient strength to excel in them.

That was the turning point. My love of sport proved stronger than the pathological obsession with slimming which had brought me to the stage where my hair was falling out and I couldn't sleep. Two years were to pass before I could bring myself to eat a potato, but I was over the worst long before then. Now I have an appetite that's almost too healthy!

While I was slowly returning to a more normal weight, Dubonnet was growing from a gangly colt into a sturdy youngster and he eventually made 15·3 hh – an inch higher than my mother's predicted limit. He was out of a Dartmoor mare and by a stallion called Golden Surprise, who was then becoming famous through another of his sons, Mary Gordon-Watson's wonderful Cornishman V. We followed the career of Dubby's relative with rising excitement – an Olympic team gold medal, the individual World and European Championships. What a star to have in the same family! Grandpa, who had bred polo ponies and was an incredibly good judge of horses, seized every opportunity to remind my mother that the horse she had been so scathing about when she had seen him first, was one of Golden Surprise's sought-after progeny.

Grandpa was no longer able to go round the local markets buying horses, because my mother had made him give up driving his Sunbeam sports car. I have an indelible memory of the last time he drove it, with my mother in the passenger seat and myself squashed in the back. We were used to his habit of turning off the engine and free-wheeling downhill in order to save petrol. The final straw had nothing to do with that; it came when he overtook not one, but two tractors with trailer loads of hay on a blind corner. 'That is *it*,' said my mother, when we returned home, thankful to be alive. 'You are *not* driving any more.'

Our interest in Cornishman's career naturally took us to the Badminton Three-Day Event as spectators. One year I saw Mary Gordon-Watson riding towards me on her famous horse, so I stopped her. 'My name's Virginia Holgate and you won't know me,' I said, 'but I have a horse called Dubonnet and he's by the same stallion as Cornishman.'

She paused only briefly, leaving me feeling a little hurt that she hadn't wanted to know more about Golden Surprise's other son. It was only later that I realised she was then doing one of the sections of roads and tracks – and that I was the thick-head who had stopped her while she was actually competing in the great Badminton Three-Day Event.

Rosemary Thomas, into whose capable hands we had delivered Dubonnet when he was still an uncoordinated colt, made another important contribution to my life. She is a wonderful character, with a great knowledge of hunting and the way hounds work, and she was wise enough to invite Pat Manning to give a dressage clinic which she had organised for riders in Devon. More important, from my point of view, she introduced my mother to Pat, who gave me a couple of lessons while I was still at school and was to reappear as my guide and mentor after I had started eventing.

I left school at sixteen, with just four 'O' levels (in English literature, scripture, history and geography) to show for my expensive education. My English language exam was a disaster. The teacher had stressed the need to be adventurous in our essays, to avoid banalities such as, 'the trees were pretty, the birds were singing and the sky was blue'. So I really went to town on an outrageous space-invaders saga and I failed with a miserably low mark of nine.

By then my parents had come home from the Philippines and settled into Ford, our house in Devon. My father, though his condition was slowly worsening, remained wonderfully uncomplaining. He took a job as warden at the medical centre in Exeter, where he organised various functions for visiting professors – meetings, lunches, cocktail parties and so on. He would drive off in a little mini which had been converted into a disabled driver's car and there was always someone to help him into his wheelchair when he arrived. He enjoyed having something to keep him occupied, so this seemed ideal.

Meanwhile Michael was still applying himself to his academic studies, in which he had rather more success than me. He was to graduate at Leeds University before taking a PhD in biochemistry at

Oxford to become a Doctor of Science. His interest in horses was far less intense than mine. Michael had no ambition to compete, preferring to potter around the country lanes on a horse, doffing his bowler hat to anyone he passed. Unless he's out hunting, he tends to believe that everything should be done at a very leisurely pace.

At the age of sixteen I was considered too young to be let loose in London for secretarial training or whatever. So, having left school after the usual exchanging of addresses and promises of future meetings, I went home to Devon.

Dubonnet was then a five-year-old. He had been broken in by a Devonshire colt breaker, who was a friend of Grandpa's. 'He'd never had a lesson in his life and the only thing he knew anything about was sitting on a horse,' says my mother. 'He didn't do any of the things that we would now regard as essential. He just got on the horse and rode it – as simple as that – and he did quite a good job. The only person who spoilt Dubby was me. I made him walk too fast, with the result that his strides became shorter and shorter. One learns from one's mistakes!'

The main thing from my point of view was that Dubby was ready to be ridden and I wasted no time in making excited preparations for our first competition, a show jumping class at our local gymkhana. I felt we looked the part – and perhaps we did – but, when it actually came to doing the job on our first public appearance, we failed miserably.

Dubby, obviously very green, started his round with zest and then took great exception to the combination towards the end of the course. He ran out once, twice, three times. Elimination! I was so mortified that I left the ring in tears.

'We'll have none of that,' said my mother. 'If you want to ride in competitions you'll have to learn to accept disappointments and be a good sportswoman.' I was angry at the time (why the hell shouldn't I cry?), but I've remembered her cautioning words since then.

That gymkhana brought me a stroke of great good fortune, as well as a salutary lesson. Sally Strachan, elder sister of Clarissa (or Clissy as most of us know her) happened to be watching and she said to my mother, 'Look, that horse has a hell of a jump, Virginia's not *too* bad, but she really could do with some lessons. Would you like to bring her over to me?'

I thought I knew what hard work was like until I became Sally Strachan's pupil. It took on an entirely new meaning under her demanding, totally exhausting, instruction. I hacked or was driven the three and a half miles to Cullompton and would then be put through the hoop of seemingly endless exercises on the lunge until every inch of me ached and I had abandoned hope of ever doing a sitting trot without bouncing to the moon and back. I can still hear her voice going through impossible demands, like a record stuck in the same groove, 'knees out, legs back, now roll the knee and thigh in on to the saddle . . .' She had told me that I would never be able to ride dressage unless I learnt to sit properly – and she was quite right – but at the time I loathed it. I only stuck with it because there was no other way of getting to the events that Sally had planned for me. It was not until much later that I began to appreciate the advantages of having my horse bend correctly, move elastically and obey my commands.

Dubby and I, two novices learning together and not an easy combination for our teacher, slowly improved. Then, having survived one form of torture, I discovered that Sally had another one in store. She and Clissy made me go to events with them and walk the course, without allowing me to ride – which, at the age of sixteen, seemed positively heartless. I must have slogged round eight or nine cross-country courses on foot, telling the two sisters what I thought of each fence and how I would ride it, before I was permitted to take my horse to an event.

It is unlikely that I submitted to all this very meekly. My mother remembers Sally telling her that I was obstinate enough to make a good competitor, but I'm not sure whether she meant it entirely as a compliment! This slow – and looking back, incredibly patient – training continued as we schooled over fences. I was expected to 'see a stride' as we approached the fence and to count them down, first from three strides out, then four, five, six, seven and eight. I can tell you, it was *not* easy!

I was still sixteen, still impatient to get started in a sport where I thought the trophies were just waiting to be handed out to me, when Sally and Clissy asked me to groom for them at the Boekelo Three-Day Event in Holland. I was totally ignorant and I can't think how they were brave enough to leave their horses – Sally's chestnut mare Parlour Maid and Clissy's By George – in my care. In all honesty, I cannot say that I enjoyed the responsibility but, as with everything else that Sally did, it was a marvellous discipline to groom at Boekelo before I started eventing myself. I reckon she was my saving grace, that few other people could have given me the discipline I needed so much at the age of sixteen and found so irksome.

I was eventually allowed to ride in my first Pony Club one-day event in the autumn of 1971. It was held locally, at Killerton, and I hacked there in great excitement. Dubby and I completed the dressage without too many embarrassing mistakes, though I don't suppose the judges found our performance particularly inspiring. The show jumping wasn't too bad either, so I was looking forward to the best part, the cross-country.

We set off with enthusiasm, jumped the first few fences reasonably well, and then the worst happened. A quarry fence that had taken my breath away on the earlier walk round loomed up ahead of us. I'm not sure why we failed to jump it – perhaps my approach was bad or maybe I was just plain chicken – but Dubby refused three times. Another elimination. It brought disappointment and anger and a furious blinking back of tears.

I rode dejectedly back to the horseboxes, loathing the thought of having to admit my failure. What would Sally say? What would my mother say for that matter? But there were no recriminations, no reminders that this was my second consecutive elimination. 'Better luck next time,' said Sally. Blow the luck, I thought, that can't do much to help such a useless rider.

But our luck did change, if only briefly. We competed in hunter trials and, to my great joy, we jumped clear rounds. According to my mother, I beamed from ear to ear each time I rode through the finishing flags with the marvellous feeling of having cleared the course.

Amazingly, Dubby and I were chosen to ride for the Silverton Pony Club team. It was a great honour and I was determined to prove worthy of it. We went to the Area Trial in Devon and my confidence grew (mistakenly as it turned out) when Dubby did a good dressage test and then whizzed round the cross-country. Our team was leading and our place in the final at Stoneleigh seemed assured when I went in for the Silverton's crucial last round in the show jumping. I must have looked like a conceited cocker spaniel as I set off to jump the first fence, unaware that I had made the stupid and unforgivable mistake of starting before the bell. It was automatic elimination, not only for me but for the whole team.

I rode out, now resembling a miserable and dejected mongrel, past the disappointed faces of my team mates. Once again my first reaction was to burst into tears and feel sorry for myself.

My mother tutored me: 'Come on, take a grip. Cheer up the other team members.' Little did I know that her efforts to teach me to control my temperament would eventually pay off. It's thanks to her tireless energy and patience that I have finally managed to subdue the fiery, emotional side of my character.

My team mates were wonderful about it, which almost made it worse because it increased my sense of guilt. I can remember looking at Dubby and wondering how such a stupid, incompetent girl had been allowed to ride such a great little horse – and I'm sure he agreed.

But life goes on. Though it took time, I managed to put my appalling mistake behind me and begin preparing, with great enthusiasm, for my first British Horse Society horse trials. They were held at Coombe Bissett and, when I walked the course, the fences looked enormous. Having inspected the Normandy bank, the coffins, hedges and stone walls, I went back to the lorry with my mother for a steak and salad lunch. With our minds still focused on those massive fences, we were both oblivious to the fact that a tea towel next to the stove had caught fire – until the lorry filled with smoke.

'Good God,' yelped my mother. *'Quick,* where's the fire extinguisher?'

I had no idea where it was (though we later discovered it in the cab of the lorry). There was much panic-stricken rushing around and banging into each other, before common sense prevailed and we used the water in the kettle to quench the fire!

Having dealt so incompetently with the fire, I had a good ride round the dreaded cross-country and finished, or so I thought, in fine style. I expected the score board to make happier reading that day but, when I went to look at it, I found a big, nasty and all too familiar 'E' against Dubonnet's name. What *had* I done this time? It didn't take long to discover that I had missed out not one, but two cross-country fences!

Another dose of mortification. My mother was pretty tired and exasperated by this stage and, if Dubby could have talked, I think the poor horse would have given me the boot and found another jockey. Sometimes I wonder how my mother has survived the amount of tension that I've put her through. I have done everything in the book that shouldn't be done – started before the bell, gone wrong in the dressage, missed out fences in the cross-country and the show jumping. You name it, I've done it.

I have always found my mistakes very hard to live with. I tend to become so totally demoralised that I end up making another error because the earlier one is still rankling. I get an enormous guilt complex at the thought of letting anyone down – team mates, those who have helped me, the horse I'm riding – and I even find it hard to look anyone in the eye while I'm going through this self-destructive feeling of remorse.

I did manage to snap out of the gloom which followed my Coombe Bissett elimination, with a successful performance in a one-day event at Wylye. Dubby was his usual brilliant self and we finished in tenth place to win our first official rosette. To this day, it takes precedence over all the others!

THREE
Junior European Championships

My next goal seemed to belong in the land of exaggerated dreams. I was aiming for a place on the British team in the Junior European Three-Day Event Championships and I worked towards it with zest — lunging, schooling, fittening work and endless practice for all the problems I was likely to encounter at the Tidworth Three-Day Event, which was also the final selection trial for the juniors.

Despite having groomed for the Strachan sisters in Holland the previous autumn, I was still pretty vague about three-day eventing. In fact, it would probably be more accurate to say that I was completely clueless.

I was tremendously grateful to have Clissy Strachan with me, because even the competitors' briefing seemed terrifying. It was impossible to absorb all the details about the flags and which side we were supposed to pass them, about the timing on the steeplechase, roads and tracks, and cross-country. A jumble of figures and, since mathematics have never been my strong point, they seemed incomprehensible.

The cross-country walk round was less complex but equally terrifying. My mother came with Clissy and me to inspect the fences and the first three seemed pretty big, while number four looked unjumpable. It was a great chasm of a ditch with a small river running through it and was called the Bourne Crossing. Having seen it, my mother said, 'That's it, I'm not going any further.' She has never even started to walk a cross-country course with me since that day, but she will usually go out and look at some of the fences on her own.

Clissy and I walked on together, with me desperately trying to absorb her words of advice. She is less than two years older than me, but she had vastly more experience at that stage. I had then ridden in only eight novice one-day events and had never jumped an intermediate course, so no wonder the Tidworth fences looked gigantic. I don't think Clissy had much faith in my ability to cope, but

33

her doubts never showed and she gave me great confidence. Even so, I was generating so much electricity that my watch stopped whenever I strapped it to my wrist. Luckily, Uncle Jack once again came up trumps and gave me a smart new stop-watch which has never let me down in fourteen years.

Dubby and I performed moderately in the dressage, which was quite satisfying considering it was the hardest test either of us had attempted. I was as nervous as a kitten on cross-country morning – even now I go through agonies during that period of waiting – and each second seemed to last an hour. Then we set out on Phase A, the first section of roads and tracks, with fears that I would get the timing wrong slowly subsiding as we met each kilometre marker on the dot of four minutes according to my stop-watch, which was exactly the right time. I hadn't a clue about the speed we should go on the steeplechase but Dubby and I sped round to finish within the time. What a relief!

Then more consultations with my stop-watch on the second roads and tracks before the ten-minute halt. I was looking forward to relaxing, to having a quiet chat about the course, but never have ten minutes gone so fast. By the time Dubby was washed down and his boots, bandages and studs checked, there was not even time to go to the loo. I climbed into the saddle, wishing that I were a hundred miles away, and waited for the countdown – five, four, three, two, one – and off we went.

My fluttering nerves settled as soon as we were on our way. A friend standing beside the dreaded fence four, the Bourne Crossing, heard someone say, 'Here comes the fat little pony,' as Dubby galloped into view – a reasonably accurate description but one that was to fill me with indignation when I was told about it later that day. While the observation was being made, I was already shouting 'Go on Dubby' at the top of my voice, all my thoughts concentrated into the determined effort to clear the monster that had looked unjumpable. My repeated exhortations must have echoed round the course. I was still yelling as we sailed over the Bourne and my friend heard the fence judge say, 'If that girl isn't in the Army, she ought to be with a voice like that.'

I galloped on, oblivious of his comments, to jump a clear round. My mother and Clissy were then forced to listen to my ecstatic account – the near misses, the wonderful jumps and the brilliance of my little chestnut horse. Dreams of completing my first three-day event were realised the next day when Dubby jumped a lovely clear round. A second dream came true when my name appeared on the short-list for the Junior European Three-Day Event Championships, to be staged

34

that year at Eridge in Kent.

The late Colonel 'Babe' Moseley, a much more formidable character than his nick-name suggests, was then chef d'équipe of the junior teams. He told my mother, in tones of severe disapproval, that I had taken a short-cut on the roads and tracks and should not have done so. 'Surely you should take any short-cuts that there are to be taken,' said my mother, who was then given a roasting for daring to express a conflicting view.

'Talk about fools rushing in,' says Mummy. 'I then said that I wanted you to be trained by Pat Manning, that I wasn't prepared to let you go to anyone else. Lizzie Boone (now Purbrick) was standing behind and urging me on, probably amazed by my cheek. 'Babe' Moseley opened and shut his mouth; I think he was too overcome for speech! Then he asked me about Pat Manning and I told him she was excellent. Although I didn't know it at the time, Molly Sivewright, who had been training the juniors, was in Australia. They were looking for someone to replace her and that was how Pat was brought in to help all those on the short-list − my daughter included!'

We had lost contact with Pat after she had given me those two lessons while I was still at school. Meanwhile Sally and Clissy had done an incredible job, but they were obviously very occupied because they were both competing themselves. 'We must have someone to teach the flat work,' said my mother, who has always believed that if anything's worth doing it's worth doing properly.

She had discussed this with Sally Strachan while I was still preparing for Tidworth and had tried (without success) to find Pat Manning's new telephone number. Then, out of the blue, she ran into Pat at a one-day event and said, 'I don't suppose you remember me?'

'I know exactly who you are,' Pat told her. 'You're Heather Holgate, Ginny's mother.'

Never slow to miss a golden opportunity, my mother asked, 'Would you be prepared to take Ginny on? She's now started eventing and we're very keen to do what we can for her.'

Pat agreed and, having mapped out the next course that my life was going to take, not even the intimidating figure of Colonel 'Babe' Moseley had a chance of altering it. There must have been times, driving me and Dubby along the seemingly endless roads from Devon to Pat's place in Slough, when my mother wondered whether she might have found an equally good trainer who lived a little closer. The motorways which make it an easy run nowadays were not at that time completed and it must have been a real pain driving me all that way and either staying a few days in the caravan or leaving me there, knowing that she would have to come all the way back to collect me a week later.

If she had any doubts (and she doesn't admit to any) they evaporated a long time ago. We both look back and realise that, just as Sally had provided what I most needed at the appropriate time, Pat was invaluable in keeping me on the right path and extending my knowledge. I went to her for years, sometimes working for my lessons and at other times paying for them when my parents had scraped enough money together or sold a piece of furniture.

I met Mandy Frank (now Mandy Lucy) at Pat's the year we were both hoping to gain a place in the junior championships at Eridge and we had a whale of a time. Dubby and I must have reaped some benefits too. Having been low in the placings after the dressage at Tidworth, we improved sufficiently to be third in the same phase during our final assessment at Wing a couple of months later.

There was great excitement when I was chosen to ride at Eridge as an individual – and when I moved into the ballet school where we were all staying for the championships. For the sake of the local residents I hope that the students of ballet, then on summer holiday, behaved better than we did.

I can assure you that the reigning individual champion, Christopher Brooke (grandson of the late Lord Brookeborough of Northern Ireland), did *not* spend all his time in solemn preparation for the defence of his title. I remember him spreading golden syrup on the loo seat, hoping to catch the Italians unawares – though I can't think what they'd done to deserve it. As it turned out, one of the British officials used the loo first and came out walking in a very odd way.

Another time Christopher was driving a mini, with me in the passenger seat next to him and Matthew Straker in the back.

'I dare you to do a handbrake turn in that drive,' said Matthew, as we were about to drive past a smart private residence.

As much of a sucker for dares as I am, Christopher swept into the drive and did a crunching turn on the gravel, whereupon the owner of the house came flying out in an absolute fury.

'Quick,' said Christopher, leaping out of the car. 'Where is the nearest hospital? My wife's having a baby.'

While I doubled up, doing my best to look the part of the wife in labour, the poor man gave hurried directions to the local hospital.

'Thank you, sir,' said Christopher, as he leapt back into the car and drove off.

A real baby was involved in my most alarming experience on the cross-country day of the Championships. The infant was in the pram which its mother was pushing behind one of the steeplechase fences just as I was coming to jump it. I screamed and she ducked in time for Dubby to fly over the fence, plus the mother and baby.

Both Christopher Brooke and I fell at the third last cross-country fence. Chris was riding that very special Connemara pony, Olive Oyl, who was originally won in a sixpenny raffle. He was on the British team, which won, the individual title going to a Frenchman, Bernard Clement. Tony Hill, son of the Devon trainer Bertie Hill, was second on Maid Marion.

Though I didn't train with Bertie Hill, I spent a fair amount of time socialising at his place. I remember seeing Mark Phillips there and, though he never said a word to me, I thought he was the best thing since sliced bread. Before his engagement to Princess Anne, I saw him at an event and noticed that the number on his back was upside down.

So I went up to him, with heart fluttering, and whispered, 'Mark, your number's the wrong way round.'

He turned round and said, 'Thank you' – and that was it. I felt terribly let down. I had expected that he would, at least, ask who I was and chat me up!

While I was competing in the Junior European Championships at Eridge, Mark was taking part in the senior event, which was also the final trial for the British and American Olympic teams which were to compete in Munich. We juniors were completely in awe of all the great riders and their wonderful horses and we watched them with mouths agape. When we looked at the names of those who had fallen at the same fence as us, Christopher and I realised that we were in incredibly distinguished company.

The bogey fence was a rail over a stream. Torrential rain had turned the bank on the landing side into a skid pad on which many horses simply lost their feet and came down. Both Mark Phillips and Richard Meade fell there, as did two of the leading riders from the USA, James Wofford and Michael Plumb. The fence had caused such havoc that the Olympic possibles competing towards the end of the day were told to miss it out.

Pat Manning had said that she would do what she could to help me gain some extra dressage marks during the short time available before we went to Eridge, but after that I would have to go back to basics. So back we went. Dubby was still only six and my mother had bought another potential event horse called Jason, who was the same age.

Both these young horses had plenty to learn, and so had their seventeen-year-old rider.

Jason had come to us the previous year from the Eggars, our great friends in Singapore, who were now living at Farnham in Surrey and providing us with a second home during the eventing season. Jason was by Pelikan, a Russian Arab stallion, and must have inherited his incredible stamina from that side of his family. His dam, Astor, was a Thoroughbred show jumping mare. Horses with Arab blood already had a fine record at Badminton. My mother can remember being thrilled when news of Richard Walker's 1969 Badminton victory on his part-bred Arab Pasha reached her in the Philippines. The horse's breeding didn't interest her so much as the fact that Richard was only eighteen. Having felt so far away, it suddenly made the ambition to have a Holgate horse competing in the great event seem less remote.

It didn't take us long to discover that Jason's powers of endurance were phenomenal. He came to us with a reputation for bolting, so we would let him take off across a ploughed field to get some of the steam out of his system. Then we felt safe to take him out on a ride.

He was a brilliant horse and he didn't stay in novices for long. In fact, in his first season as a five-year-old, he won a section of the intermediate class in the Army One-Day Event at Tweseldown. That took place a couple of months after the junior championships at Eridge and it was an unforgettable day since I won the other intermediate section on Dubonnet. With marvellous riders like Mark Phillips, Princess Anne and Jane Bullen (now Holderness-Roddam) behind me, my head was in danger of getting too big for my cap.

It was after Tweseldown that we put Jason on the lorry with Dubonnet and took him up to Pat Manning's for the first time. Pat asked to see him trot in a circle and he promptly fell over.

'You don't want to buy that horse,' Pat warned us.

'I already have,' said my mother.

'I see,' replied Pat. There was nothing more to be said.

At that time I still had one more year left before I would be too old for the junior team and I was determined to make the most of it. Dubby and I were a bit more clued up when we went to the 1973 Tidworth Three-Day Event, where we finished second in the junior trial behind Sara Bailey on Red Amber. Both Sara and I were selected for the junior team which went to Pompadour in France.

We stayed at the Club Mediterranée and, as far as I'm concerned, it was magic. It was like being in a five-star hotel, with amazing buffets and a wonderful swimming pool into which the all-girl British squad was continually being thrown. The Russians earned a reputation for nicking all the bananas in the buffet before the rest of us arrived, so much so that word went around that the Russians had never seen a banana before.

The first inspection of the cross-country was a pretty alarming experience. We all thought the fences were vast. Colonel 'Babe' Moseley, our chef d'équipe, kept insisting that the bigger it was the better it suited us. 'You can jump it,' he said, 'but what will happen to the others?' As he admitted afterwards, it was a very tough course for juniors and much more in keeping with an event of Badminton's stature. We were known as 'Babe's babes' and the strong young lads from the eleven other nations represented didn't think we had a chance.

Pat Manning was there to give us invaluable help with our dressage before we faced the terrors that lay in wait for us on cross-country day. I was last to go for the team, and one of our riders, Dawn Brands, had already been forced to withdraw. Her Just a Cloud, the best of the British after the dressage, was stung on the dock by a horsefly while waiting to start and he went completely berserk, falling over a wire fence in his panic. It was hoped that he might recover on the first roads and tracks, but the horse was completely shattered and Dawn had no option but to pull him out.

The roads and tracks brought some problems for me that day. Trotting gaily along and trying to stay calm, I waved to a family having tea in their garden. Having waved back, they suddenly leapt out of their chairs screeching, 'Non, non mademoiselle,' and pointed in the opposite direction to the one I was taking. I looked round to see that the kilometre marker, which had fallen against a hedge, agreed with their directions. I was en route for Paris!

Returning to the ten-minute halt, my instructions were to ride carefully. I had to get round in order to have the necessary three members of the team still in the contest. I did my best to obey the instructions. Dubby and I managed to scrape round without any penalties, and the pathetic-looking team of 'Babe's babes' was well in the lead at the end of the day. Sara Bailey, who had beaten me at Tidworth, was lying first in the individual and I was second, less than one fence behind.

I am not a patient person and waiting has always seemed painful. The long wait until it was my turn to show jump on the final day is one of the most difficult I can remember. By the time I went (in programme order rather than the present-day reverse order of merit) Sara's Red

Amber had dropped a foot in the water, leaving me with a chance of winning the individual as well as a team gold. Dubby obliged by jumping a clear round for victory.

There were champagne celebrations afterwards. My Uncle Jack was very chuffed when he persuaded the Poles to drink some with us, while I revelled in the genuine pleasure that was conveyed by all those who had helped towards my success. Grandpa, of course, made the most of this latest opportunity to remind my mother of her derogatory question ('What did you want to buy *that* for?') when he had just purchased Dubonnet from the Five Lanes Cattle Market.

FOUR

Mini-Olympics in Montreal

I returned home from France thinking I was the bee's knees, the junior title having really gone to my head. At our next competition, a one-day event at Ermington in Devon, I listened smugly while the announcer told everyone, 'This is the reigning Junior European Champion, Virginia Holgate.' Then I fell flat on my face – not once, but twice – over a simple show jumping course.

The first mistake was with Dubonnet, who tried to do a two-stride double on only one stride and landed splat in the middle of a parallel, the second element. I remounted and finished the course before coming back with Jason, who was bursting with excitement because he had just set eyes on a huge white mountain dog. He wasn't concentrating and neither was I; he gave a huge jump over one of the fences and off I came again. Having remounted once more, with the swollen head somewhat reduced in size, I jumped over the same fence again, instead of going on to the next one, and was eliminated.

I have to admit that it served me right. It was a timely lesson in what horses can do to you when you become too big for your boots. By the time I started preparing Dubby for my first ride at Badminton, in the spring of 1974, I was in a more suitably humble frame of mind.

Meanwhile, I had also failed miserably when trying my hand as a waitress at the Cullompton Hotel in Devon. As luck would have it, I started work on a day when they were holding a big dinner and dance in the hotel, where I was kitted out in black, with white apron, cuffs and collar. I was then given a tray stacked high with bowls of soup and told to hand them out around the table. Terrified that I was going to drop the lot, I kept my eyes on the tray and managed to miss the table with one of the bowls, sloshing hot tomato soup all over a lady's black velvet dress.

Realising that I was a menace with a stacked tray, they gave me a single gravy boat to take round for the second course. 'All you need to do is pour a little gravy on everyone's plate,' they said.

Somehow a rather large blob of gravy managed to land on a man's ear and drop to his immaculate white collar. I was sent to the kitchen to wash up after that and, by now a nervous wreck, I promptly broke two plates. Paying for the damage cost me more than my day's wages and my job was terminated – by mutual consent.

I felt on safer ground looking after the horses in the three cattle sheds which served as stables during our early years at Ford. In addition to Dubonnet and Jason, there was now a third occupant whom I had starting eventing. This was Tio Pepe, a dark brown Thoroughbred gelding bought by my mother in 1969 as a yearling. I had been dragged around with him in the Land Rover and trailer during his early years, while we were showing him in in-hand hunter classes at various big agricultural shows, such as the Bath and West and the Royal Cornwall. He was quite successful, but I'm afraid I found it all very boring.

My interest in Tio Pepe's impact on the judges only took off when he became old enough for novice eventing. He was undoubtedly the most handsome of the three horses and a really exciting prospect for the future. We used to put him on the lorry with Dubby and Jason for that long journey to Slough, where I was still going as often as possible for lessons with Pat Manning. I would never have progressed without her help.

We had become good friends with Dorothy Willis, Pat's head girl, but were still in awe of Dot when it came to 'her' yard. As luck would have it, Pepe caused a great deal of trouble on his first day there. To begin with he dug up a deep litter bed that had been laid six months earlier, then he escaped from his stable and led us a merry goose chase round and round the yard.

One of Pat's great strengths is that she teaches the rider, not the horse. It would have been an easy short-term solution for her to get on Dubby or one of the other two horses and iron out any of the problems, but she was aiming to teach me how to train them myself. I owe her my grateful thanks for persevering in that much more difficult task.

Pat has never taken the easy option. If, for instance, the horse's head was too far to the right, she wouldn't say (as some trainers might) 'Turn the horse's head to the left.' She would be more likely to say, 'The reason that the horse's head is turning towards the right is because your right hip is too far forward; put it back.' Ten to one, you do what she says and the problem is cured.

There were moments of extreme frustration during the hours Pat would spend asking me where I thought I'd gone wrong and how I felt a particular problem should be overcome. I wanted *her* to give *me* the answer, not to be asked to apply my own brains to the problem. But, looking back, she was doing me an enormous favour. Now I have Dorothy Willis, who worked with Pat for years, to help me. But there are still the odd occasions when I ring Pat and say, for example, 'The horse is tilting to the left, what would you recommend?' She can then ask whether I've tried this or that. We know each other so well that we can actually sort out a problem over the phone.

By 1974, while preparing for my first Badminton, I had also started going to Lady Hugh Russell for cross-country schooling at Wylye. She has been invaluable to me over many years, and to virtually everyone who has ridden for Britain in the last decade or so.

Going 'up to the top' at Wylye meant riding up the long hill to the bare and windy stretch of Salisbury Plain, where a marvellous variety of fences had been built. Lady Hugh would follow in the famous mini-moke which she had started driving after breaking her back in a hunting accident. For the passenger, staying in Lady Hugh's vehicle when she is in hot pursuit of a horse is a feat in itself. She had put dots of paint on the combination fences (Lady Hugh's spots as we called them) which was to show us the correct line. You had to jump where the dots were for the distance to be correct − a foot to the right or left just wasn't good enough.

She had a great influence on my ability to see a good line through a combination fence and to keep the horse going straight as I ride through it. I still see imaginary dots on the fences when I walk a course now and, because of her training, I have the confidence to tackle some of those difficult lines where you have to be perfectly straight and absolutely accurate.

Lady Hugh thought the world of Dubby, though there were times when he really frightened her. He had a tendency to stand off a long way back from a fence and she had visions of him landing in the middle of it, as he did when helping to knock the conceit out of me after I had won the junior title. But he had a tremendous leap and rarely had any problems in clearing single fences from far away.

I was preparing for Badminton with the help of a training schedule which Sally and Clissy Strachan had drawn up for me. It was the system that had always worked for them and, since I hadn't a clue about getting a horse fit enough for the biggest annual three-day event in the world, I was immensely grateful for it. At that time I weighed less than 8 stone, which meant that Dubby would have to carry a substantial amount of lead to bring us up to the required minimum of 11 stone 11 pounds.

It would have been lovely for my trainers if their nineteen-year-old pupil could have been among the prizewinners at Badminton in 1974. But I'm afraid my only claim to fame (having been frozen with fear after walking the cross-country) was not of the kind to impress anyone. I happened to be on the course at the same time as Richard Meade and, because of that, I appeared on television. The picture switched from Richard to this young whipper-snapper in purple colours on a little chestnut horse and the commentator said, 'Virginia Holgate has jumped Huntsman's Leap and she's gone – yes I'm afraid she's gone into the bushes.'

They switched to Richard and showed him jumping five fences on Wayfarer and then returned to Holgate. A little purple flash mingling with the bushes revealed that I was still trying to find my way out of the copse on the far side of Huntsman's Leap. After I had slipped my reins as we jumped the fence, Dubby had gone charging into the bushes – and, by the time I had got myself organised and back in control, I was lost. Richard had jumped seven fences before I found my way back on to the course.

After this embarrassing experience, which included twenty penalties for going outside the penalty zone, Dubby ran out at the Star three fences later. It was entirely due to rider's error; I had totally the wrong line. Apart from that we were clear and I did have the satisfaction of completing my first Badminton, though I was never the slightest threat to Mark Phillips, who won on the Queen's Columbus.

Later that year I had the chance of returning to France, this time with Jason, as one of the senior riders competing in the Haras du Pin Three-Day Event. The 1969 European Championships (won by the British team and, individually, by Mary Gordon-Watson on Cornishman V) had been staged there and some of the fences which alarmed riders of vast experience were still in use. I gaped at them in disbelief, as did my team mates, John Kersley, Angela Tucker and Merlin Meakin. Lady Hugh was there and she told me that she was bringing a marvellous picnic with her for cross-country day and that I would be welcome to join her as I was unlikely to get past fence two.

Dick Carpendale (who was there with his wife, Helen, to watch John Kersley ride their horse, Sporting Print) was probably less interested in the course than the fact that he had lost two front teeth shortly after his arrival, while biting into some chicken. John also forgot about the fences on the night when Stuart Stevens, another Devonshire event rider, who was there as a groom, played a wicked prank on him by locking him out of the lovely château where we were all staying. Wearing only his underpants, John had to climb across a moat and wall, then sneak back in through another door, hoping that he didn't meet anyone en route. In fact he did meet Mr Carpendale, who stared at John's scant attire. It seemed pointless to try and explain the reason why he was just in his underpants and some distance away from his bedroom, so both mutually decided on less said, soonest mended.

In the end I didn't share Lady Hugh's picnic. Jason, still only eight, was not nearly as overawed as I had been when he saw those huge fences for the first time (including the original Normandy Bank where I closed my eyes and prayed from a field away) and he jumped a bold clear round. It was a great thrill when we finished the event in second place behind the French Olympic rider, Domini Bentejac on Aragon.

We were stranded in France for five days on the return journey, waiting at a village called Honfleur, near Le Havre, for the gales to cease so we could take the horses back across the channel. My mother and I slept in our caravan, which the Carpendales had been towing behind their Land Rover, and we had run out of French money by the time it was calm enough to sail with the horses, who were travelling in the Russell's lorry. Our final meal was an unappetising-looking mixture of the last tinned food in the caravan store: chicken, apricots, baked beans and sweetcorn. Stuart Stevens (who always looked as though he needed a square meal and was nicknamed Toast Rack for obvious reasons) said he would rather die of starvation than eat such a revolting mixture but, after we had commented on the delicious flavour, he quickly joined us and ended up consuming more than anyone else.

The following year, we offered Richard Meade the ride on Jason for the 1975 Badminton, and he accepted. I already had Dubonnet to ride and since I had only competed at Badminton once before, my mother thought it would be too much for me to try taking two horses there. Anyway, Richard didn't have anything to ride and Jason was really more of a man's horse.

We did some cross-country training together at Wylye, with Lady Hugh, and I can remember Richard having a slight hiccup at one of the fences. Jason didn't fall, but he missed his stride and only just managed to clamber over. Lady Hugh said, 'That won't do at all, you'll have to talk to him the way Ginny does when you come into a fence.'

So Richard entered into the joke and came out with a pathetic high-pitched girl's voice, squealing: 'Come on Jason.' Everything went beautifully after that.

Our training began to seem a bit pointless when, after weeks of rain had made the ground in Badminton Park impossibly soggy, the great event was cancelled after the first day of dressage. But I was soon given other goals to chase. Tio Pepe, then aged six, did his first three-day event at Tidworth the month after Badminton's cancellation and he went really well through the mud and pouring rain to finish second, encouraging our high expectations for the future. Two months after that I took Dubonnet to the French Championships at Haras du Pin, where I had finished second on Jason the previous year.

France had also been hit by the wet weather, and the sweltering sunshine that replaced it on cross-country day only served to make the ground as sticky as glue. I was first to go for the British and I made the fatal mistake of going too fast on the steeplechase; under conditions like that you should expect to get time faults. Poor Dubby did his best to overcome my error of judgement until he fell on to a bank, the second part of a double, on the cross-country.

He caught his stomach as he fell and then lay winded. He eventually struggled back on his feet and I remounted, but I knew that he wasn't right and didn't want to go on. As I was riding for Britain, I chose to let him circle three times and be eliminated instead of withdrawing – though, as it turned out, no one could have blamed me for pulling out since poor Dubby proved to have internal injuries.

The other members of our team went brilliantly. I had been the only Briton in the top six the previous year, this time I was the only one who didn't get into that top half dozen. Diana Thorne (now Henderson) won on The Kingmaker, with Jane Starkey fourth on Topper Too and Mandy Frank sixth on Touch and Go III.

I was feeling very depressed about Dubonnet's injuries, but knew that I would have to shake myself out of the blues very quickly. Before we left for France, an invitation had arrived asking whether I would like to ride Jason in the Mini-Olympics at Montreal later the same month. I had jumped at the chance and Sue Hole was now at home getting Jason ready for the Canadian challenge. As it turned out, through problems with some of the other horses who were due to go, I was the only British competitor, with Richard Meade as my own personal chef d'équipe!

I flew out to Canada with Jason and had a wonderful trip, acting as air hostess to the pilot and crew. We might have enjoyed ourselves a little less had we realised that part of the engine had fallen off on the

46

journey, but fortunately it was not discovered until we were safely back on land.

The Montreal police were having a test run of the security which would be in operation for the full-scale Olympics the following summer. This inevitably meant that we had difficulties in getting from place to place but we still had great fun at the various parties given for the riders. Jimmy Day, who was to make history the following year by riding in both the Olympic show jumping and eventing teams for Canada, became my hero, though I doubt whether he knew much about it, since he only danced with me once and to my distress treated me just like a kid.

My dressage test came very close to being a total disaster. The time for it had originally been set for 2.30 pm, so I had planned an early lunch with the idea of getting on Jason at 1.30. Then I was told there had been a hold-up and my dressage time had been put back to 3.00. This seemed fine by me, since it meant I could enjoy a leisurely lunch.

I was still sitting at the table at 1.30 with Richard Meade and my mother, when a call came through to say they hadn't needed to put the times back after all and that my dressage test would be at the original time of 2.30. Talk about panic. It took about a quarter of an hour to drive to the stables and, by the time I got on Jason, it was so late I had to trot him all the way to the dressage area, while he got more and more wound up.

There was scarcely any time to prepare my horse for his test. By then he was giving an excited attempt at piaffe (unasked) with his tail high in the air. Richard told me it would be pointless to go through any of the movements with him. 'All you can do is rising trot until you start the test,' he said.

It was obviously sound advice, since Jason was leading from the 34 other horses at the end of the dressage. I think the judges must have been impressed by his tremendous forward impulsion which resulted in him recording the fastest time of the day.

Richard was a tremendous help to me throughout the Mini-Olympics. He walked the cross-country course with me in a thoroughly professional way, kept an eye on the horse's fitness and so on. He couldn't have been more helpful. I did my best to follow his instructions and was glad he wasn't watching when I made a real hash of the water on cross-country day.

This nasty moment came towards the end of the course, at a bridge in the middle of a lake. There was a small rail to jump coming off the bridge and I don't think Jason saw it. I came within a hair's breadth of falling off as he struggled to regain his feet, but we somehow managed to stay together and go on to complete a clear round within the optimum time. It was that day I made a vow never to eat a cooked breakfast on a cross-country morning. The sausages I had eaten played havoc with my concentration as I burped my way around the course.

I had 14 points in hand as we went into the show jumping. In those days a single show jumping error cost 10 penalties (as distinct from the present five) so we could afford only one mistake. One fence fell but, thank heavens, we cleared the rest. The thrill of winning was made even more perfect by the fact that Jimmy Day (my hero) lined up beside me for the presentation, having finished second on Mr Superplus. The kid had beaten the big shot!

For the second time I returned home from an overseas event thinking that I was God's gift to the world of three-day eventing and was soundly put in my place by a horse. This time it was a private humiliation. Since I was so superb across country (or so I thought) I dared myself to jump a big hedge at home. Jason cleared it safely, but I fell off. It was another timely reminder to say, right mate, that'll teach you not to get too conceited!

Before Christmas that year I took a job at Harrods, where I did my best to sell ties, while my feet ached and I sweltered in the unaccustomed hot-house atmosphere. Some of my customers were delightful and others were appallingly rude. One of the former kept returning to listen to my limited sales talk; there is not really much you can say about a tie once you have commented on its colour, but this particular customer made a purchase each time. He must have bought about eight ties before I went out for a drink with him. His name was Simon Wilson.

'How long have you worked in Harrods?' he asked, thinking it was my permanent job.

I explained about the horses and we had a general chat about sponsorship. Then he said that he might be interested in owning a horse, so it was arranged that he would come to stay with us in Devon for a weekend. He didn't buy an eventer, but he has remained a close and valued friend of the family since that visit.

In addition to my temporary day-time job at Harrods, which lasted about five weeks, I was working in a wine bar near Paddington during the evening. Wondering why the money wasn't piling up, it eventually dawned on me that my wine bar earnings equalled the cost of getting to and from the place by taxi. Being a dolt at mathematics, it took me three weeks to work out that simple equation.

FIVE
A smashed left arm

I celebrated my twenty-first birthday in February 1976 with a fabulous party given by Uncle Jack at his home in Kent. About six weeks later I broke my arm in twenty-three places. The accident happened at the Ermington One-Day Event in Devon, where I was giving Jason one of the outings that was supposed to prepare us for Badminton. We were on the long-list for the Olympic Games and I was eager to impress the selectors that spring.

The fall was entirely my fault. It was a very hilly course and I knew Jason was in need of a breather. But I kept him galloping up a long hill to a one-stride double, where (so I'm told) someone ran across the course about 20 yards ahead as Jason was jumping the first part. It could be that the horse was tired or that his attention was distracted by the running spectator.

Whatever the cause, Jason left one leg on the wrong side of the second fence and turned over. As I went flying through the air, I put my left arm out to break my fall and failed to bend my elbow. So the impact of the fall smashed my wrist, then Jason landed on top of me and knocked my elbow out of place. The whole arm had been rotated so that when I sat on the grass, wondering what injury I might have done myself, the elbow was pointing up instead of down.

'I think I might have broken my arm,' I said to the friends who came rushing up to ask whether I was all right. I was taken to the ambulance where everyone had a big discussion over whether I should be driven to Plymouth or Exeter, while they sat around drinking cups of tea.

'Do you think I could have a cup of tea?' I asked, plaintively.

'No,' I was told, very firmly. 'You can't have a cup of tea, because you might need a general anaesthetic.'

They went on drinking their own cuppas, which I thought was very mean. Who needs tea? I don't even like it, I thought, scowling. My moment of great importance would however come, I imagined, when the journey began and they put on the siren. But we crawled slowly and silently to the Plymouth Naval Hospital, where it had been decided to take me, with our friend and neighbour, Lesley Fraser, to accompany me while my mother dealt with the horses. I was still dressed in all the gear – crash helmet, jersey and number, breeches,

49

boots and spurs. The poor nurse who received us at the hospital was clearly disconcerted by this apparition; I think she imagined that I was wearing the latest craze in motor-bike gear.

They took me to the theatre pretty smartly for an operation which apparently lasted four hours. I came out of the anaesthetic the following morning to find my arm in plaster and suspended from a hook. I thought it didn't look too bad even though I couldn't move my thumb or fingers. I lay there wondering how long it would be before I could ride again.

Commander Bertram, who was surgeon at the Royal Naval Hospital, took a more serious view of the injury. He had told my mother that nothing could be done, that all the nerves had been damaged and my arm would probably have to be amputated from just above the elbow. Horrified at the thought, she asked if he could save it, even if it were to remain paralysed and therefore useless. She also rang Simon Wilson, the friend I had met while working in Harrods, to ask whether he knew of anyone who could give a second opinion. He swiftly arranged for me to be seen by Dr Lawrence, an eminent orthopaedic surgeon at Guy's Hospital, but, in the meantime, Commander Bertram had decided that he would try to reassemble my broken bones.

It was fortunate for me that the long deliberation over cups of tea, which I had so much resented at the time, ended with the decision to take me to Plymouth. Commander Bertram was probably the only surgeon in the country who would have attempted that formidable task. In another four-hour operation, he somehow managed to put the broken jigsaw in my arm back together, with the help of pins and screws. When we showed Dr Lawrence the X-rays, he said that the surgeon who had managed to save my arm was nothing less than brilliant.

Returning from that visit to London, we called in to see Pat Manning and Dorothy. I was amazed and tremendously touched when Dot put her arms round my neck and I noticed the tears streaming down her face. Little did I realise how much I would come to rely on her loving wisdom in the years to come. Nowadays I never walk a cross-country course or do an important dressage test without her at my side. She has spent hours lungeing our horses; she has watched my every move in the saddle, using her knowledgeable eye and practical common sense to foster my progress in three-day eventing. As well as all that, she has helped me through my many moments of self-doubt with patience and understanding.

I was in and out of hospital that spring and had a total of five operations. I also learnt to count my blessings through encountering a young girl with Parkinson's disease and a poor old lady, who had broken both her legs a year earlier and was still in hospital with both limbs encased in plaster. My problems seemed minuscule by comparison and, after talking to them, I used to think to myself: you don't appreciate how lucky you are.

As I was incapacitated, we asked John Kersley (then my current boyfriend and a very talented horseman) to ride Jason at Badminton. My great ambition, the dream that kept me going, was to see my horse compete in the 1976 Olympics in Montreal. But it was not to be. The day before he was due to go to Badminton, John gave Jason his final gallop at Pat Manning's place and he had another ghastly nose-bleed. We had no alternative but to retire him from eventing.

My own future in the sport looked equally doubtful. I had been told there was little likelihood of my being able to use my left hand again, that I could possibly get some feeling back in my elbow, but even that was doubtful. The elbow had been set so that my arm was fixed in a right angle and my chances of ever being able to straighten it were, as I was also told, extremely remote. I was advised to get a car specially designed for disabled drivers.

Commander Bertram wisely left the rest up to me. 'I'm not going to send you to a physiotherapist or suggest any exercises,' he said. 'You know what you can do. The nerves are crushed very badly, especially the main nerve, and you're not likely to get any feeling back, but it just might happen. If it does, you will know what to do.'

It was about two months after the final operation when I first felt a tingling sensation in my fingers. It was a moment of enormous excitement. A bit of feeble movement returned and I set myself a daily task of trying to undo a button on my right sleeve. It took me forty-five minutes, except on a few occasions when I cheated by flicking the sleeve up instead of wrestling with the button, usually to the accompaniment of some colourful language.

Then I gave myself a new target. This week, I'd say, I'm going to pick up a toothbrush. The next week I'd try something heavier. And so it went on, day by day and week by week, the excitement of knowing that movement was slowly returning set against the frustration of realising that I couldn't possibly hold a rein in my left hand. I had an ambition to ride Tio Pepe at Burghley that year, six months after my accident, which undoubtedly helped me to persevere in trying to use the hand.

Slowly but surely, I reached the stage where I could pick up a glass and take a sip from it. My main problem then seemed to be the bent elbow, which I couldn't straighten. Occasionally I would try to force it straight, which hurt like hell and failed. Then one day our vet, Don Attenburrow, came to see one of the horses. I showed him my X-rays, which had done the rounds of the universities because they apparently gave a fascinating example of what could be done with smashed-up limbs. After studying the X-rays, Don took hold of my left arm and, quite literally, yanked it straight. It was momentarily very painful, but that was nothing compared with the immense relief in having it back to a normal position. Since then Don has become known as the Guru.

It is still not quite as straight as most people's left arms, and I can't turn it so that my palm is flat enough to accept change at the shops, which can be embarrassing when coins trickle to the floor!

I am, of course, by no means unique. I'm just one of the people with a story to tell about an injury. I'm also one of the lucky ones; my minor problems don't amount to a handicap. Whatever strength you need in your arms for riding comes from the shoulder and I have no weakness there. I can hold a horse – or, for that matter, carry a suitcase – because my shoulder rather than the lower part of my arm takes the strain. In short, I am very fortunate.

About five months after the accident, I rode Dubonnet in a couple of open intermediate classes at one-day events to try and regain confidence in my ability to ride a horse across country. He put me back on the right path by giving me good safe rides. Thanks to Commander Bertram's amazing surgery, I was to fulfil my ambition to ride in the three-day event at Burghley that year on Tio Pepe, the potential star of our stable.

Tio Pepe was very talented and highly intelligent, though we didn't much appreciate his repertoire of tricks at home. By now my mother had bought five looseboxes to give us some extra stabling and, since Tio Pepe had learnt how to unlock his door, we always had to secure his bolt with a special catch. Sometimes we forgot.

On one occasion we had invited some friends for Sunday lunch and happened to look out of the window as we were tucking into our meal in time to see a loose horse walk by. Then a second, third and fourth went past.

'What in heaven's name is going on?' yelled my mother, completely bewildered by this succession of horses, who should have been safely locked up in their stables. We were too isolated for any stranger to have come strolling in and opened all the doors.

The mystery was solved when we found Tio Pepe in his stable, with the door closed but not bolted. He had let himself out, unbolted all the other doors with his teeth and then returned to his own stable where he pulled his door shut. He was standing there looking a picture of innocence while our lunch guests, unsuitably dressed as they were for a Devonshire round-up, helped us to catch the loose horses.

The story may sound far fetched, but it was totally in character with those of us who knew Tio Pepe. He was permanently treading on our toes and would always contrive to move a few steps forward so that he caught you twice, first with a fore foot and then with a hind foot. If you put a blanket on him and then turned to pick up the rug which was to go on top, he would whip the blanket off with his teeth during that brief instant when your back was turned. He was the most infuriating horse I've ever come across.

He was also liable to get up to a few tricks during dressage, but he was a super jumper and very bold across country. He gave me a tremendous ride that year at Burghley, though I found it difficult to follow my mother's instructions to go slowly on the steeplechase course, in order to conserve Tio Pepe's strength in the very deep ground. I was also terribly rusty and it was the horse who helped me out of trouble at quite a few of the cross-country fences that we reached on an impossible stride. At one big parallel he stood off such a long way back that I was told a concerted gasp of horror was heard around the closed-circuit video screens, as everyone anticipated a hideous fall. But Tio Pepe flew over it and completed a clear round.

My arm was feeling very sore when I rode him into the show jumping arena the following day. I couldn't use the left rein effectively and had to form a bridge with the reins, so that my right hand could be used for steering left as well as right. It was hard to concentrate under these circumstances, which is the only excuse I have for missing out a show jump and getting myself eliminated yet again.

My mother was fuming; I have never seen her so angry. It was purely frustration on my behalf, the fact that she had watched my efforts to be fit enough to ride at Burghley come to nought, that caused her to blow her top. It was not for her sake, but for mine, that she had longed to see me put the problems of the year behind me by completing Burghley and I was on my way to doing just that when I made my stupid mistake. Since that day I have made a point of walking the show jumping course of any three-day event until I know it blindfold, usually at least four times. This has not gone unnoticed by youngsters who write to ask me why I walk the course so often. The only answer I give them is to explain about my past errors.

That winter I went to work as personal assistant to Jeremy Hamp in his company, London Video. I had met him through his wife, Angela (who was an event rider) at a time when I was anxious to find work in London but didn't fancy returning to a sales counter at Harrods. Jeremy told me he needed someone to help and it didn't matter if I couldn't type – he would be willing to take me on as his personal assistant. I did manage to type the odd letter for him, each of which took me about two hours, while my adding up of the accounts seemed to show a different total at each attempt!

His company was making training films and my initial job was to set up sites for the videos to be made. After about a month he decided he could use me as an actress as well, so I appeared as the customer to whom the various complexities of whatever merchandise we were filming had to be explained. It was much more fun than selling ties or working in a wine bar. Brigitte Bardot eat your heart out!

I was given time off in the December of 1976 in order to go to Ireland. Pat Manning had been asked to give a series of lecture/demonstrations, which were designed to show the Irish that flat work really did help to improve a horse's jumping. Pat was to deliver the lecture and I was to ride the four horses, who included Dubonnet. The other three were a mixed bunch – Fiona Reeve's Ballinkeele (who had been short-listed for the Mexico Olympics), a Grand Prix dressage horse called Sallachore (who was trained by Edith Masters) and Sea Mist (owned by Sir Frank Taylor, who sponsors dressage).

It was agreed that Pat and I would fly to Ireland, while my mother drove the horses in our lorry, with Linda Blanchard (who worked for Pat) following behind in a car in case Mummy ran into trouble. What she did run into was thick fog on the motorway, and she had a nightmare journey to Swansea where they were due to catch the boat to Waterford.

'The fog was so bad that I tried to get off the motorway at the exit before the Severn Bridge,' she says. 'But I missed the exit and decided I might as well press on. I was a nervous wreck by the time I eventually reached Swansea, so much so that I insisted on talking to the captain because I wanted his assurance that we weren't going to have a bad crossing on top of the dreadful drive. I told him that he could count my lorry out if we were likely to have a rough trip, but he insisted that there wouldn't be any problems. How wrong he was.

'It was by far the worst sea crossing I have ever experienced in my entire life. Linda, who had been following me in the car, was far too ill to be of any help, so I had to stay with the horses in the lorry. I didn't dare leave them. Every vehicle on that lower deck moved and I was terrified, I still don't know how the horses managed to stay on their feet. Every so often the captain would send someone down to see whether I was still alive and he did apologise for the inaccuracy of his forecast, but that didn't make it any less horrendous.'

Pat and I heard about my mother's ordeal when we joined her in Waterford, where the first lecture/demonstration took place. We then drove across Ireland to Galway for our next performance, which went well. I think we managed to persuade our audiences that flat work wasn't a total waste of time, though we did overhear the odd comment from people who suggested that all these fancy horses might not last too long if they went hunting in Ireland! Some of those watching must have been reasonably impressed, since Pat was later asked to train Ireland's junior three-day event riders.

We left Galway on a bright and frosty morning to drive to Iris Kellett's marvellous riding school at Kill, near Dublin, where we were to give our third and final demonstration. My mother and I travelled in the lorry with the horses, while Linda once again followed by car. Mummy, who is a very careful driver, was diligently watching the roads for any patches of ice and she had established the comforting fact that the puddles weren't frozen when we came slowly round a sharp bend and the lorry suddenly went out of control.

'Every time I drove the lorry out of one skid, the weight of the horses took it off in another direction,' says my mother, who remembers it in vivid detail. 'We did half-passes all along the road and then went over an Irish bank, the two of us instinctively leaning back with our feet stuck forward as though we were out hunting. As we landed in the field, my concern was to keep the lorry upright. There was a moment of great relief as we landed on all four wheels, but then the weight of the horses took us over.'

Needless to say I can also remember the horror as the lorry toppled on to its side. My mother told me in a normal matter-of-fact voice to switch off the engine, then she had to hoist me up so that I could reach the door, which was now above my head, and clamber out. The lorry, thank God, had a canvas roof and we found one horse's head sticking through it, while another was calmly munching hay. We ripped the thick canvas with difficulty and dragged out the horse whose head was through the canvas. Then my mother went in to untie the other

55

horses. One of them kicked her in the face and, to add to the horror of the scene, she started bleeding.

Dubby was next on the stack of horses and somehow I managed to find the strength to pull him out by his tail. It was slightly easier to get the remaining two horses out and on to their feet, by which time Linda (who had driven to the nearest cottage for help after seeing the lorry land on its side) had returned in a state of frenzy, not knowing whether we were dead or alive. The people who came with her were standing on the bank blessing themselves as they witnessed this extraordinary scene. Each horse had a tiny cut over one eye and another over one knee; amazingly enough, these were their only injuries.

To add to the chaos, Linda's car was in collision with another victim of the ice. The man who had driven into her was upset and angry until I pointed to the field and he saw the overturned lorry, which made his own problem seem insignificant. I then took the dented car and my mother's wallet to go and telephone for help and, still dazed by the shock of our crash, left the wallet on the roof of the car so that my mother lost her money and credit cards.

Eventually the police arrived and a doctor, who was wonderfully kind to us. He lived about five miles away and, since the lorry was a write-off, we walked to his place, leading the horses through the bitter cold and along seemingly endless icy roads. The horses were put into stables, while the doctor and his wife produced cups of coffee for us and contacted Pat Manning by phone to tell her what had happened. Iris Kellett very kindly sent her own horsebox to collect us and we had thawed out by the time it arrived an hour and a half later.

To our surprise, the horses seemed to be totally unaffected by their alarming experience. All four walked into Iris Kellett's lorry without the slightest hesitation and Dubby performed the same evening, as though nothing out of the ordinary had happened. He loved showing off and, though he has never been a particularly good mover, was always very accurate in his dressage and usually got a reasonably good mark for it. So he was useful in these demonstrations since he did good flat work despite the limitations imposed by his action – and he had a terrific jump.

The hospitality in Ireland was wonderful, and so was the food. We had no idea that the restaurants there would be so incredibly good and, despite the traumas, we did full justice to all the delicious meals. Since our vehicle was wrecked, Iris Kellett nobly sent the horses back to England in her own lorry. We had no means of transporting our horses for several months after that trip, but we had to be thankful for our own survival.

My mother has been very wary of horseboxes ever since. She blamed herself at the time, feeling that there must have been something she could have done to prevent us hurtling over an Irish bank. She has since spoken to many lorry drivers and they all say the same thing. If you are carrying anything that moves – whether it's milk or sheep or horses – there is nothing you can do once you hit ice and start skidding. Remembering that the only possible way we could have extricated the horses was through the roof, we now travel with a mallet and axe in case we ever need to break open the solid roof of our present vehicle.

By the spring of 1977 my hopes of impressing the selectors of Britain's senior team rested with Tio Pepe. Jason had already been retired from the sport and we subsequently sold him to Duggie Bunn, of Hickstead, where we hoped he would remain. Much to our sorrow, Duggie sold him on to Holland and we learnt that he had started eventing again, despite his history of nose-bleeds. Dubonnet had been retired from senior three-day eventing, because we had decided that the minimum weight was too much for him to carry.

So Tio Pepe was to be my ride at Badminton that year and we went through the usual three months of preparation, only to meet with another bitter disappointment when he broke down on the steeplechase course. I was left in gloom and despair. In little more than a year I'd smashed my arm and seen my three advanced horses pushed into early retirement. I thought it was all too much for anyone to bear.

A long time of despondency and indecision was to follow. I had been going out with John Kersley and we had discussed the possibility of marriage, without reaching any firm conclusion, when he moved to Canada that year. I was praying that the Good Lord would direct me on the right path while I toyed with the various possibilities. At one stage, I packed a trunk to go out to Canada and see the place where John was living, but then changed my mind and unpacked again. I'm sure it was right that I didn't go – both for me and for John, who later married a Canadian.

Having unpacked my trunk, I dithered over the idea of giving up eventing and trying to start a new life in something completely different. Meanwhile I rode in some one-day events on a lovely six-year-old mare called Abbey, bought by my mother, without resolving my future plans. Some welcome relief from these weighty considerations came with an invitation to go to Burghley, immediately after the 1977 European Championships had been staged there, to be considered for a riding part in the Film *International Velvet*.

I duly lined up outside the Burghley Horse Trials office with the other event riders who had been invited. Equity, the actors' union, also had some riders there, having insisted on sticking to the terms of an agreement which supplied work for its own members. It was a weird arrangement, since it meant that each star of the film who was supposed to be seen riding across country had a look-alike Equity member to be filmed in the sequences on the flat between fences, and another look-alike event rider to do the jumping.

The Equity people had already been chosen and I luckily resembled one of them, Jan Gaye. I was therefore among those chosen by Bryan Forbes, the film's director, as we stood in line outside the Burghley office. The other event riders who took part in the film included Jane Holderness-Roddam, Richard Meade, Diana and Jane Thorne, Stuart Stevens, Alistair Martin-Bird, Nigel Tabor and Julian Seaman. Another of the extras was Georgina Simpson, now married to the actor, Anthony Andrews, who was responsible for dressing some of the actors through her family's firm, Simpsons of Piccadilly. Commander John Oram was in charge of us all, helped by the United States Olympic show jumping gold medallist, Bill Steinkraus, who instantly became my new hero!

The story was basically about Sarah Brown (played by Tatum O'Neal) and her ambition, which is eventually realised, to ride in the Olympic Three-Day Event. Tatum learned to ride remarkably well, but she obviously couldn't do all the sequences on Magic Lantern, who was Sarah's horse Arizona Pie in the film.

Jane Holderness-Roddam riding Warrior (with a white star painted on his forehead and with his snip and white socks removed with carefully applied chocolate powder) doubled for Tatum in the cross-country jumping. I doubled for her in some of the dressage and show jumping scenes on Magic, and also in a beach sequence which was shot in Devon. According to the script, Sarah Brown is galloping across the sands when her Aunt Velvet (played by Nanette Newman) comes to the top of the cliff and waves a telegram which has arrived from the selectors. So at a given point during that gallop across the beach, I had to throw an arm in the air and shout, 'Yippee,' – which is my one and only claim to fame on the screen.

For the cross-country jumping I rode my mother's mare, Abbey, with my look-alike Equity member riding her between fences. We were both playing the part of an American three-day event rider. It was quite a test for Abbey, who was still only a six-year-old intermediate eventer, since she had to jump some of the Burghley fences. I'd be sitting having coffee when the call would come, 'Right you riders, we want you to jump the Waterloo Rails in ten minutes' time.' We had one show jump to warm up over, then had to jump one of the toughest of the Burghley cross-country fences. That part was quite nerve-racking but the rest was enormous fun.

We were staying at the Bull Hotel in Peterborough, where we had marvellous à la carte meals each evening and happily left MGM to pick up the enormous bill. After we had finished filming at Burghley everyone moved to Arena North, near Preston in Lancashire, for the dressage and show jumping sequences. It had been hoped that a huge rent-a-crowd would arrive, lured by the prospect of earning £5 a day and seeing the stars in action, but the weather was foul and the crowd looked a bit thin for an Olympic audience. So life-size cardboard cut-outs of people were cunningly used to give the impression of a vast audience.

It was obviously a great thrill to meet people like Bryan Forbes and his wife, Nanette Newman, Tatum O'Neal, Anthony Hopkins, Christopher Plummer and the American actor, Jeffrey Byron, who later invited me out to Los Angeles. Nigel Dempster actually wrote a piece in the *Daily Mail*, complete with photographs, which said that Jeffrey was involved in 'a little real-life wooing off the screen . . . I can reveal that his real belle is Virginia Holgate, 22, ex-Junior European three-day event champion.' The piece appeared out of the blue. Mummy and I giggled and thought fame at last, the gossip column true to form.

Meanwhile, I was lapping up the wonderful opportunity to see a feature film being made, while being paid for the privilege. I was to share a flat in London with Bryan Forbes's daughter, Sarah, after we had finished filming and I had gone back to work for Jeremy Hamp at London Video for a second winter. Jeremy let me take a couple of weeks off for my trip to Los Angeles (which was not recorded by Nigel Dempster!), where I stayed with Jeffrey Byron's delightful mother, Anna Lee (who was one of the nuns in *The Sound of Music*) and her author husband, Robert Nathan.

The will-I-won't-I continue in eventing was still unresolved in the spring of 1978. I knew that Abbey would have to be sold, because my parents were broke and she was the only animal in the yard who could fetch a high enough price to solve the financial problems. I had a new boyfriend called Philip Moseby, a money broker without the remotest connection with horses, and my recent disappointments in the sport were still rankling.

I was very close to giving up when I started schooling my mother's two five-year-old horses, who were due to make their eventing debut that year. Their names were Night Cap and Priceless.

SIX

Two new horses

We had spied Night Cap in a field about a mile away from our home while he was still an unbroken youngster and we thought he was smashing. He was owned by John Chapel, who had bought him as a yearling, and we were anxious to have a closer look at him if, and when, he was up for sale.

'If you feel like selling the horse, do let us know when you've backed him,' my mother had said to John. 'We'd love to see him down at our place.'

So one day John turned up riding Night Cap, who was going sweetly for him. 'What about jumping?' we asked.

'Oh, he's able to jump all right,' said John.

We pointed to a very nasty ditch and said, 'How about jumping that?' Night Cap flew over it without a moment's hesitation.

'When did you back him?' my mother asked.

'I just got on him this morning,' said John, nonchalantly.

Before she bought Night Cap, my mother phoned up Dorothy Willis (who was then head girl at Pat Manning's yard) to say she had seen a young horse she liked but was a little worried because it had rather a lot of knee action.

'Don't let that worry you,' said Dot. 'It means the horse will jump.'

By then Dot was making the odd journey to Devon to give lessons. She came as a result of my mother, in desperation after making all those long journeys with me and the horses to Slough, phoning Pat Manning to say, 'Is there any chance of you coming down here. I'll get some other people for you to teach as well, so as to make it worthwhile.'

Pat was too busy to come herself, so Dot came instead and my mother managed to get one or two extra people, who were keen to have lessons and helped to pay for the expense of bringing an instructor to Devon. Our training took place on the top of a high hill that was covered in chicken manure – no wonder there was a shortage of boyfriends! It's a far cry from the present luxury of our outdoor school provided by John Latter.

Dot liked Night Cap as soon as she saw him. He is by Ben Faerie, the stallion at Diana Scott's stud in Somerset. My mother's love of buying horses later prompted her to enquire whether there were any other youngsters by the same stallion for sale. Diana said that she had only one, a five-year-old horse she had been using as a hunter. So off we both went to see him. We liked the hunter and bought him.

Our new purchase was Priceless, so aptly named by Diana's sister when she saw him as a new-born foal and said, 'What a priceless little thing!' We put him into the horsebox with Night Cap and took him up to Pat Manning's yard, where Dot looked him over. 'You can sell that straight away,' she said. 'He'd be quite nice as a riding club horse, but that's as far as he'll go.'

My mother was poleaxed. 'We'll show you,' she said, huffily. She has never let poor Dot forget that day.

Mummy has inherited Grandpa's instinctive talent for buying horses, and his addiction for it. She can remember someone asking, while she was still in her teens, what it was that her father looked for in a horse and saying, 'I don't suppose he knows.' Like him, she relies on an instinctive feeling rather than technical judgement.

Also like Grandpa, who was a genius at buying wonderful horses without parting with much money, my mother loved bartering. 'I think the family must have been gamblers at some stage,' she says. 'Buying horses is a form of gambling and it's like a drug to me.'

She is willing to travel hundreds of miles to see a horse and regrets that the days of bartering are past, now that there are too many people chasing after the few good horses that come up for sale. Dot also loves buying horses. She looks at them in a technical way, while my mother is relying on instinct, and it's obviously a good combination. But (if she will forgive my saying so) I'm glad Dot wasn't around when we bought Priceless.

I was still close to quitting the eventing world when Lucinda Prior-Palmer (now Green), who knew I was feeling very low, invited me on a young riders' seminar that she was giving at Wylye. 'I know you don't qualify as a young rider any more, that you're now an old codger,' she said, 'but why don't you come along?'

I suggested that everyone would think it a nonsense to see me appear on the scene, but she brushed the objection aside. 'Never mind what they think, you come along anyway.'

So I took Night Cap and Priceless (N and P as I call them at home) to

Wylye for the week. These two five-year-olds, both waiting to compete in their first novice one-day event, were as different in character as chalk and cheese.

P has always been very independent. You can't tell him anything, because he reckons he knows it all. When you do interfere, he tends to give an enormous buck just to let you know who's boss. Bridget Maxwell rode him when she was helping with the dressage at Lucinda's Wylye seminar, and she fought a losing battle in trying to make him more submissive. He bucked every time she asked him to canter and, when she gave him a whop to tell him that he was to stop his bad behaviour, he bucked again. So she gave him another whop and he retaliated with another buck. And so it went on. Every time she used her stick on him, Priceless would as good as tell her to shove off; he wasn't going to listen to anyone telling him what to do.

Eventually, Bridget said, 'I think perhaps we'd better try something different because this is obviously not going to work.' So she stopped using her stick on him and he stopped bucking.

If Priceless were human, he would have made a good sergeant-major. He'd be butch, short, muscular and aggressive. Night Cap is much more the officer type: incredibly polite, very good-looking and far more sensitive than his bossy stable companion.

Lady Hugh Russell, who built up such wonderful training facilities at Wylye, was at home during the young riders' seminar and I grabbed the opportunity for a cross-country lesson with her. After watching Priceless jump, she told me that she liked him: 'He's very bold and he has a good brain.'

Lucinda was less ready to be drawn when I asked for her verdict on P. 'I don't know yet, let's wait and see how he goes at novice level,' she said. I suspect that she secretly wondered whether he was a bit too common to make a top-class eventer, but she diplomatically refrained from saying so.

That seminar was the turning point for me. I shall always be immensely grateful to Lucinda for helping me to turn a difficult corner and putting me back on the right road. By the end of the week I was thinking: how dare you be so sorry for yourself. If you want to give up by all means do so, but for heaven's sake stop thinking that you've had a raw deal.

My father also became one of Lucinda's fans. He rarely saw me competing because he was usually working, but he did manage to get to a local one-day event at Bicton. He came in his wheelchair and Lucinda, without knowing who he was, went across and talked to him. It was only after chatting for a while that she discovered he was my father. Afterwards he always described her as 'a wonderful person'.

The novice section of the Taunton Vale Horse Trials was Priceless's second event. Still a precocious five-year-old, he was absolutely determined that he knew best and that the person on top didn't have a clue.

We were haring down a hill towards a double and I tried to tell him that he needed to slow down, otherwise he would fall over. I was all too well aware that there was very little space between the two fences, and it was therefore necessary to be slow and accurate. But P refused to listen to my signals, he knew best. I saw a long stride, but realised it was the last thing I wanted; if we jumped off a long stride, we would land straight into the base of the second fence. So I sat still and closed my eyes.

Priceless was about to take a flyer at the first part of the double – from the stride that I had seen and rejected – when he noticed there was a second fence. He tried to put in a short stride, but was going too fast and therefore turned head over heels at the first element of the double. I landed on the second element and broke the top rail.

P climbed to his feet looking suitably shocked. He was certainly not going to suffer from an anxiety neurosis as a result of the fall, but it did occur to him that it might be worth listening to his rider in future. I remounted and he completed the course, jumping better than ever before. From that day on, he has taken notice when I ask him to slow down – or to shorten or lengthen his stride – but he's still prepared to tell me who's boss if I try interfering in any other way.

He has also made it perfectly clear that he is not going to stand having any bit in his mouth which might give me the feeling that I am in total control. When we tried him in anything stronger than the mild Dr Bristol snaffle, which I always use for cross-country and show jumping, he simply dropped the bit – refusing to accept contact through the reins if I was going to have too much of a say in the speed we went.

The gentlemanly Night Cap was much more obliging that day at Taunton, when he won his novice section. So was the wonderful Dubonnet, who was second in the open intermediate. Though we never asked Dubby to compete at Badminton again, I did return there with him to do some stunt riding for a film called *The Great Event* which followed the fortunes of Jane Holderness-Roddam and Chris Collins. My contribution was to canter between the fences with a

1a. By all accounts I was a bit of a monster . . .

1b. With my mother and first pony, Misty

2a. Riding Dubonnet in far from elegant style (*Findlay Davidson*)

2b. With the wonderful Dubonnet I won the Junior European Championships in 1973

3. No hint of the troubles in store.
Riding Jason at the 1976
Ermington One-Day Event
a few fences before I smashed my arm
in twenty-three places
(*Kit Houghton*)

4a. Diana Scott and Ben Faerie, the sire of Priceless, Night Cap and Murphy Himself (*Kit Houghton*)

4b. Night Cap on his way to winning the Advanced class at Dauntsey Park in 1980 (*Kit Houghton*)

4c. Badminton, 1981. Priceless competing in the great event for the first time to finish eighth (*Kit Houghton*)

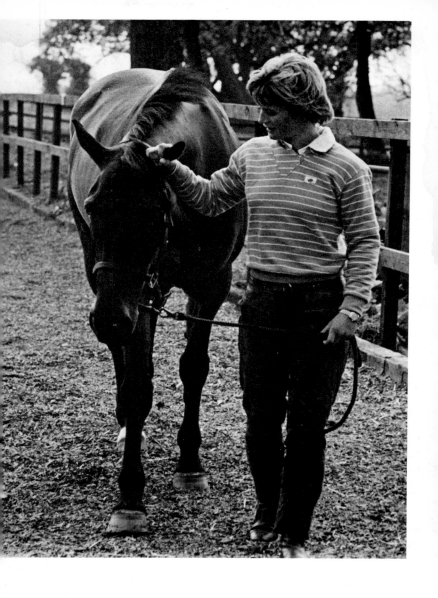

5. At home with Priceless
(*Kit Houghton*)

6a. Frauenfeld, 1983. Malcolm 'Minder' Wallace tries to maintain calm as Night Cap and rider wait to start the cross-country (*Kit Houghton*)

6b. Badminton, 1984. Night Cap looking confident, despite his horrific nose-dive seven fences earlier at The Lake (*Kit Houghton*)

7a. The British Olympic team wearing the Union Jack shorts bought by Ian Stark and Robert Lemieux (*left to right*): Tiny Clapham, Lucinda Green, Ian Stark and myself (*Kit Houghton*)

7b. Waiting to hear my score after the Olympic dressage with Malcolm Wallace, chef d'équipe, showing signs of anxiety (*Kit Houghton*)

8a. On the Olympic steeplechase course with Priceless (*Kit Houghton*)

8b. Priceless cools down in front of a fan while my mother and Clare Tweedie prepare him for the Olympic cross-country (*Kit Houghton*)

camera strapped to my crash helmet giving a rider's eye view of the obstacles.

Having finished, I rode across Badminton Park looking like a martian and, quite by chance, ran into Prince Charles who was out for a hack. He asked me what I was doing with a camera strapped to my head and we rode on together while I explained all. Later we decided to jump a log near the Grandstand, first on our own horses and then (having swapped mounts) on each others.

'Will you be at the ball tonight?' asked Prince Charles before we parted. Already bowled over by his charm, I eagerly assured him that I certainly would. Queen Virginia here we come, I thought, as I dolled myself up in excited anticipation. Alas, it was all for nought. I had read too much into his polite enquiry and, having looked for him in vain at the ball, realised that he hadn't meant he would be there himself! I'd better stick to horses!

By then Tio Pepe had recovered from his tendon trouble and had been lent to Ewan McCrae, with whom he became a Grade A show jumper. Sadly, he broke down again during 1984 and had to be put down. Abbey was sold to Germany in 1978 and before we lost touch we heard that she was placed in a couple of three-day events there, which pleased us enormously. There was never any question of parting with Dubonnet (except to lend him to Richard Meades wife, Angela, for hunting) and he is still with us.

With my mother's backing, I enjoyed a fair amount of success in novice classes with Night Cap and Priceless. Mummy has never ever pushed me, which must make her angelic as the parent of a rider – or, for that matter, of any youngster in sport – and a shining example to most of the others. She hasn't refrained from giving me hell if I did something stupid, like lose my way in dressage or wherever.

But she has never put any pressure on me to win an event. All she has ever wanted is for me to do my best and, as long as I do the job to the best of my ability (without any stupid mistakes), she is perfectly satisfied, even if I finish last.

Another person who has had a great influence on my life is Pat Burgess, to whom I first went for show jumping lessons in 1981. She achieves incredible results with tin cans and other apparently makeshift equipment in a field beside the railway line at Wilton near Salisbury, where she is the devoted trainer of a large Riding for the Disabled group. She has also helped all the senior three-day event riders, teaching us at Wylye during the final training sessions (the concentration camps, as I usually call them) before all the major championships. She has a wonderful knack of giving the horse tremendous confidence in its jumping ability through exercises over grids and lines of small related fences.

Perhaps most important of all, Pat and I share a firm belief in God. The prayers and biblical quotes she has sent me over the years have always been relevant to my state of mind and therefore a great source of comfort. One year she even sent me a religious quotation to read on the loo during the ten-minute halt at Badminton – and I followed her instructions to the letter!

I was petrified of making one of my stupid errors when I took Priceless to his first three-day event at Bramham in 1979. He was only a six-year-old and, because he had more pony character than Night Cap was that bit more advanced of the two horses. In a sense it was silly to take him to Bramham when he was still so young, but he'd gone well in a few intermediates and I was eager to do another three-day event, my first since losing my way in the show jumping at Burghley almost three years earlier.

There had been a 'double bounce' (the Lexington dog kennels) at Badminton that spring and, before I left for Bramham, I was crazy enough to decide that I must teach Priceless how to do one. So I built three fences, fondly imagining that they were the right distance apart for him to pop in and out without any non-jumping strides. Priceless knew better and he ran out three times before we had even reached the first element. I was distraught, convinced that both of us were useless and that we were bound to have a disaster at Bramham. In fact, I had made the distance far too short, with about 4 yards instead of 5 or more between the fences, and Priceless was wise enough to know that I was asking the impossible. I did my best to put this experience behind me as I set off for Yorkshire.

Because it was so long since my last three-day event, I felt as though I was starting all over again at Bramham; I thought I was bound to go wrong on the steeplechase or on the roads and tracks, to say nothing of the dressage, cross-country and show jumping. I watched the steeplechase for about two hours and made four trips around the roads and tracks (to the detriment of the car) before I rode over them.

Priceless gave my confidence the boost it badly needed by winning Bramham, which was an incredible thrill. I would have been even more livid than usual if I had made a mess of it, because I missed my brother's wedding (which took place the previous weekend) in order to compete there, and my mother rushed back just in time to drive us to Yorkshire. Michael and Fiona were married on Stronsay Island in the Orkneys and my father was able to travel up, with my mother and Uncle Jack, for the wedding. They reckoned it would have been quicker and far easier to have flown to New York, having changed planes in Aberdeen and (after a terrifying flight in dense fog) in Kirkwall on the mainland of Orkney. A tiny plane took them on the last hop to Stronsay.

They said the journey was well worth it. The wedding (at which Michael, to my mother's horror, wore his hobnail boots) went on for three days, with fiddlers playing and everyone on the island joined in the celebrations. My parents were delighted with the whole scene and with their new daughter-in-law.

My father thought the world of Fiona. She had worked for the BBC on outside broadcasts for *Nationwide* and has since produced some of the Russell Harty programmes. She, Michael and their son, who was born in 1985, live on Stronsay – not far from the island of Auskerry, which Michael owns jointly with the former manager of The Who pop group, Simon Brogan. Michael occasionally works as an engineer on an oil rig, but the rest of his time is spent in more leisurely pursuits such as tending the sheep, fishing for lobsters in the Orkneys and, believe it or not, knitting.

By the time of the wedding, my father had moved into a tiny bungalow, purpose-built for him with the help of a government grant beside the main house in Devon. He hated being pampered, so the place was specially kitted out for him in order that he could fend for himself. We also had a tiny heated swimming pool installed, which he used virtually every day. Since he was confined to a wheelchair and couldn't walk, swimming gave him the exercise he needed. He valued his independence and the fact that he still had a job at the medical centre; he would have loathed having nothing to do. My mother and I saw him regularly and we usually had our evening meal together, which Mummy cooked and took to the bungalow.

I left for a holiday in Greece immediately after winning Bramham. Philip Moseby and I had been invited there by Mike Rutherford (who is part of the group Genesis) and his wife, Angie, both of whom have since become good friends of mine. Apart from the frequent necessity of digging needles out of my toes (I seemed to stand on every sea urchin in the Greek waters), we had a wonderful time, made extra special for me because of the Bramham result. There was further encouragement on the eventing scene that autumn, when Priceless and Night Cap went really well in their first advanced contests at Tetbury and Chatsworth one-day events. Things were really looking up.

In May the following year, I took the two horses (now aged seven) to the Hooge Mierde Three-Day Event in Holland, where I nearly made one of my unforgivable blunders on the steeplechase course. It was one of those figure-of-eight courses they often build on the Continent and I was concentrating so hard on the way I was riding that I forgot the route. I had to pull Priceless up and stop while I debated whether to continue on round in a circle or whether this was the point where I should take the diagonal route across the figure-of-eight.

There was a man standing about 10 feet away from me looking pointedly towards the diagonal and, in the belief that he was trying to tell me something, I went charging off in that direction, hoping and praying that it was the right one – which it was. I managed to finish the steeplechase just one second within the optimum time.

Lord Hugh Russell was there as our chef d'équipe and he was waiting for me when I reached the Box on Priceless for our ten-minute halt before the start of the cross-country. I was still wondering how I could have possibly been so stupid when Lord Hugh said, 'Now, about the steelpechase Ginny . . .'

I stopped him as swiftly as I could. 'We will *not* discuss that at this particular moment, Lord Hugh, if you don't mind.' I was feeling far too angry with myself to go through the mortifying details.

Priceless did a rotten dressage at Hooge Mierde, but he was super across country and finished in twelfth place. Night Cap had a fall at one of the ditches (a natural hazard on the cross-country course and not part of a fence), where he twitched a nerve in his shoulder and was lame for a few minutes during which time we retired, though he was thankfully all right.

Burghley was the next big goal. The trip to Holland had shown that Priceless had masses of ability across country and I was impatient to take him to one of the major three-day events. I rode him at Burghley in the September of 1980, a little less than four months after he had competed at Hooge Mierde, and this time he did a good test – he was actually in the lead after the first of the two days of dressage, much to our delight and surprise.

Not wishing to push my luck on such a super young horse, I took him fairly steadily on the cross-country, but we still finished in sixth place. It was wonderful to line up for the prizegiving, feeling that I was now one of the 'big boys'. At the head of the line, from first to fifth, were Richard Walker, Mark Phillips, Jane Holderness-Roddam, Beth Perkins (USA) and Lorna Clarke. Having scraped into the top six, I was taken off to a tent with them to drink champagne and be presented with a lovely cut-glass decanter. I was into the Big Time.

My bubble burst later that evening when I went to the George Hotel. A couple of people told me that I had a jolly nice little horse, with a huge jump, but that Priceless couldn't gallop and would never be able to go fast enough to get within the optimum time. They probably don't even remember making those comments, but I was deeply hurt.

I'll show them, I thought. As it turned out they did me an enormous favour in galvanising me into a furious attempt to prove them wrong. They were not the only ones to hold this view; few people at that stage shared the Holgate belief that Priceless really was priceless. But it was a very painful jolt to my soaring expectations.

A few weeks later I took Night Cap to the three-day event at Wylye, where we finished second to Phoebe Alderson on April's Dancer. Looking across to the spectators during the presentation, I suddenly spotted my father in his wheelchair, holding a tiny bottle of champagne and beaming from ear to ear. It was the only three-day event in which he ever saw me compete; I had not expected him to be there and I was so thrilled, and so overcome, that I burst into tears.

At that stage we were in the process of selling Ford. Our lovely house in Devon was too big and expensive to maintain; it was also a desperately long way from most of the events I was going to with the horses. My mother had put in a bid for Ivyleaze, at Acton Turville, one mile from Badminton, together with the bungalow behind the main house whick seemed ideal for my father. He was still living in Devon, carrying on with his job and taking his daily exercise in the swimming pool, while my mother was motoring back and forth between the two places. Then he contracted pneumonia and was taken to hospital, where my mother was a frequent visitor until he made a remarkable recovery and returned to the Devon bungalow, with a live-in nurse to take care of him until he was fit enough to move to Ivyleaze.

Meanwhile, I had been invited on a return trip to the Philippines, to give lessons to the Pony Club. I had been there for about two of the three weeks I was due to stay when I began to wonder why my mother hadn't phoned; it was unlike her not to call and say; 'Hello, how are you?'

I also remember waking up in the middle of the night and thinking to myself that I must write my father a really long letter. There was no particular reason why I should have done so; I'd already sent him a post-card. But it seemed imperative, so I sat down and wrote about fourteen pages to him. A few days later it seemed equally necessary to phone home. When I got through, my mother told me that she had been trying to ring me for several days, because my father had died on 13 December.

I was totally shattered. I wanted to get home as quickly as possible after receiving this devastating news on a Thursday night, but found I would have to wait until the following Monday before making that sad flight home.

My mother had been seeing my father almost every day on her fleeting visits to Devon. Then one day she phoned him to say that she was on her way and he told her that he wasn't feeling too brilliant and would rather she left it until the following day. She therefore reluctantly agreed to delay her journey.

My father died that same day. He was in bed, cracking jokes to the nurse, before taking a deep breath and dying. My mother was terribly upset at not being with him, but it may have been the way he wished to go.

I wanted to mourn for him equally quietly. But, as I had discovered during my uncomfortable year as a schoolgirl in Manila, the customs of the Philippines are very different from those in England. People couldn't understand my desire to get away and be on my own during that weekend when I was longing to return home.

It seemed impossible to explain all this to the people with whom I was staying, which made the loss of my father seem even more painful. It was a relief when Monday came and I was able to fly back home for the funeral.

SEVEN

European Championships
at Horsens

By the time of my father's death it had already become apparent that I couldn't continue to event unless I could find a sponsor. At that stage only a few of the top riders were sponsored and I was a little pip-squeak compared with people like Lucinda Prior-Palmer, Mark Phillips and Richard Meade. Nevertheless I put my best foot forward, first writing to companies and then going out and knocking on doors. No one seemed to have the slightest interest in backing me. I was told that the budget was already allocated, that eventing wasn't really their scene, all the usual polite ways of saying that they really weren't interested. They would wish me luck and off I'd trudge with my portfolio to bang on the next door.

The position seemed hopeless as I prepared Priceless for his first Badminton in the spring of 1981. By then Dorothy Willis had moved in to live with us at Ivyleaze and become a regular and valuable part of our team. She had been a freelance instructor since Pat Manning changed her yard some time earlier and she used to visit us quite frequently. Eventually my mother suggested she should live at our madhouse and freelance from there.

People said it would be a disaster. My mother, Dot and I are three fairly strong personalities and everyone thought we were bound to clash. But it has worked wonderfully well – mainly, I think, because we all have quite separate parts to play and no one interferes in anyone else's role. We are a real team.

My mother sees to schooling and breaking the youngsters. She copes with the early fittening work for any of the horses we are preparing for a three-day event and many a time has come in from road work literally freezing. What makes her determined to help to the degree she does is a miracle in itself. She is also responsible for the all-important feeding and is therefore chief chef for both humans and horses. I school the horses for competitions, which involves flat work, jumping, cantering and galloping. Dot is in charge of all the equipment, of lungeing the horses and helping me with my flat work.

I might be on one horse while Dot is lungeing another in our outdoor school. So I can say to her, for instance, 'I'm not sure that this shoulder-in is quite right.' She'll tell me what adjustments I need to make and we'll both carry on as before. As a rider you have to have someone knowledgeable on the ground, who can see when something isn't quite right and can help you to correct it.

Having worked together, Dot and Pat Manning (who are still great friends) are remarkably similar in their methods of training. If you were given typescripts of what each one had said during a lesson, it would be impossible to tell one from the other. I still have some help from Pat; she'll come down before a big event like Badminton or Burghley and I occasionally take a horse up to her for some concentrated training, but otherwise I rely on Dot.

There is a wonderful – and sometimes hilarious – relationship of mutual respect between Dot and Priceless, each one knowing that they can't go too far. If either of them does overstep the mark, there's likely to be a swift comeback. I can remember Dot admonishing Priceless at an event one day; he was tied to the side of the horsebox and was irritating her by pawing the ground.

'That's enough of that, Priceless, for heaven's sake stop it,' she said, giving a yank on his rope.

He waited until her back was turned and promptly retaliated by giving her an enormous butt with his nose, which sent her flat on her face.

Louise Bates, who was (and still is) my great buddy, was riding Colonel Jack at Badminton in 1981, the year I first took Priceless there. I had met her through another friend, Ginny Thompson, who was third at Badminton back in 1973 on Cornish Duke. Louise and I have had some riotous times together and she frequently acts as my 'minder' in times of stress, as will be mentioned later.

That year Priceless gave me a wonderful ride and we finished eighth. We would have been fifth but for 5.25 penalties in the show jumping and, though it was galling to drop back three places, the result was still exciting, especially as we had gone fairly cautiously on the muddy ground across country, without attempting many of the faster and more difficult routes. Priceless was still only eight and I was tackling those awesome fences for only the second time, without having greatly distinguished myself with Dubonnet on the first occasion some seven years earlier. Neither P nor I were ready to tackle the route taken by Mark Phillips for his win on Lincoln.

Immediately after Badminton, I redoubled my efforts to acquire sponsorship. I even went to Mark McCormack's International Management Group and asked, 'Please will you help me to find a sponsor?' They were charming – they gave me a cup of coffee, patted me on the head and suggested that maybe they could do something 'another time'. In other words, they couldn't help me. It still seemed hopeless.

Then one day Simon Wilson (the friend with a large collection of Harrods ties) said he had heard of a firm called British National Insurance that was sponsoring someone in sailing. 'It might be a complete waste of time,' he warned me, 'but why don't you ring Mr Miller, who's the managing director, and see if he'd be keen on sponsoring an event rider?'

I promptly phoned Mr Miller, who told me that it was out of the question; his firm would not be able to help.

'Oh come on,' I pleaded. 'You can't just turn me down over the telephone. At least meet me and let me tell you something about myself.'

He relented sufficiently to agree that he would meet me for lunch at the Inn on the Park the following Thursday.

'How will I recognise you?' I asked.

'I'm bald and fat,' he said.

Feeling that I should also be recognisable, I told him that I would wear a mac. When Thursday came it brought a baking hot summer day and my 007-style beige raincoat looked ridiculous. Sweltering, and feeling uncomfortably conspicuous, I went into the Inn on the Park and found about a hundred bald fat businessmen there. How on earth was I to find Mr Miller amongst this lot?

I took a deep breath and went up to the nearest of those who looked as though they might be waiting to meet someone.

'Excuse me,' I said. 'But are you by any chance Mr Miller?'

'I'm afraid not,' he answered and, obviously thinking I was there on the pick-up, added, 'but do let me buy you a drink.'

I had approached about five bald fat men – and they had all responded in a similar vein – before the real Mr Miller stood up. He was neither bald nor fat. He had been having a whale of a time watching the conspicuous woman in the mac giving everyone the wrong impression. You toad, I thought, that's the last time you're going to play one of those tricks on me.

The tables turned when, after lunch and several glasses of wine, Gordon Miller found himself agreeing that he would talk to his chairman, William Samengo-Turner.

He would let me know the outcome in three days. As luck would have it, Mrs Samengo-Turner was very keen on horses and I suspect her interest helped to sway the balance in my favour. Anyway, the telephone call came to say that they agreed in principle and that we would have to arrange a meeting to settle all the details at a later date. I can't tell you the excitement this produced at Ivyleaze.

Meanwhile I had been short-listed with Priceless for my first senior European Three-Day Event Championships, to be held at Horsens in Denmark, and was anxious to prove my worth to the selectors as well as to my future sponsors. My first effort towards achieving this goal was in the final trial (staged during the Midland Bank Championships at Locko Park) and it was not particularly clever. I came down the centre of the arena at the start of my dressage test, made my halt and salute, and then couldn't remember whether I was supposed to turn left or right. With a fifty per cent chance of getting it right, I still managed to go the wrong way. The dreaded bell rang to indicate an 'error of course'. To rub salt in the wound I noticed the chief selector, Chris Collins, standing a few yards away and watching with an eagle eye.

Fortunately the penalty for one lapse of memory during the dressage is not severe. This one was forgotten (or forgiven) thanks to Priceless, who ended up winning the final trial. It was a wonderful thrill when I was chosen to ride in the British team, with Richard Meade on Kilcashel, Sue Benson on Gemma Jay and Lizzie Purbrick on Peter the Great. Rachel Bayliss on Mystic Minstrel and Tiny Clapham on Windjammer were chosen as individuals. We all travelled with the horses, spending the lengthy sea trip eating far too much, then driving across Denmark confident that our horses would enjoy the flat terrain. Little did we know that the competition ahead was set in the one and only hilly part of Denmark.

Confidence turned to apprehension when I had my first look at the cross-country fences they had designed for us in Horsens. Even the experienced riders regarded some of them as unjumpable and, after the first walk round, I was a nervous wreck. I was still reeling from the shock of inspecting those fences when our chef d'équipe, Major Malcolm Wallace, asked me whether I would be happy to go first for the British team. I gulped at the thought of taking on such a formidable responsibility in my first senior European Championships.

'I'll go first if you think I'm capable,' I said.

'Yes, I think you are.' Malcolm (or Wol, as we were to call him as we became more familiar with our chef d'équipe) sounded reasonably convincing. So I kept my reservations to myself and agreed.

On the same day, Colonel Frank Weldon, president of the ground jury in Horsens, emerged from the meeting at which the order of starting had been drawn, and gave me a wicked grin.

'You're first to go,' he said.

'I know I'm first to go for the team, Malcolm's already told me that,' I replied.

'Not just first for the team,' said the Colonel with a chuckle, 'but first to go in the competition.'

'You're joking,' I suggested. But this was no joke, I really was to be first of the sixty-one competitors to go out and tackle those terrible fences.

It was no help at all to return to the agricultural college, where all the riders were staying, and feel a sense of desperation in the air.

This was on Wednesday night and, being first to go in the entire competition, I was to do my dressage at 8.30 the following morning. It was not the time to dwell on the hazards to be faced on Saturday's cross-country. The immediate concern was to make sure I knew the dressage test and didn't lose my way again.

The next morning there was a thick fog and I couldn't even see the judges' boxes as I entered the arena, which presumably meant that they couldn't see me either. Afterwards I wished that they could have seen me better, because I thought Priceless did rather a good dressage test and was therefore disappointed with his low mark. The multiplying factor, which is used to make the dressage marks exert the right influence on the whole of the competition, was high (at 1.5) because of the severity of the cross-country course. So I was 30 points behind Rachel Bayliss, who was leading on Mystic Minstrel, at the end of the dressage.

While the others were doing their tests, I was concerning myself with further inspections of the cross-country course. Tiny Clapham and I were walking round with Richard Meade, when we came across Sue Benson in a state of despair.

'Don't worry,' Richard said, 'We won't be riding over the course as it is at the moment.'

I was totally flummoxed, especially as we'd been firmly told that a local rider on a 'rural' horse had successfully negotiated the entire course! Surely the fences had already been passed by the technical delegate, Anton Bühler from Switzerland? How could any changes be made at this late stage?

Yet Richard seemed convinced that the four fences which looked suicidal to us riders would not be included in their present form. The chefs d'équipe from the fourteen nations taking part were eager for changes to be made and on Friday afternoon we were told that modifications had been agreed. We were so overjoyed by the news that we opened a bottle of champagne beside fence fourteen, the silver birch rails which stood at the top of a steep slide and were now (much to our relief) to be lowered. A real party started. I've never seen anything like it – celebrations *before* the event had even started.

Despite the alterations, I was apprehensive when I woke early to another morning of thick fog and set out for the stables, where my mother was staying in a caravan. The horses were living in a tent, with Priceless at the entrance to act as guard-dog because he threatened to eat anyone who passed him. I noticed the worried faces of my mother and Dot as I went into the caravan to change, in nerve-racked silence.

Priceless was led out by Karen Priddy-Smith, who was grooming for me, and I climbed on to prepare for my awesome responsibility as first member of the British team. Malcolm Wallace was there to see me start on the first roads and tracks, no doubt aware that my nerves were jangling. 'There's no need to worry,' he said. 'We know you'll do your best and, whatever happens, we'll still love you when you come back.'

I'll never forget those words, because they made all the difference in the world. I was desperately anxious to prove myself as a good team member, to jump the steady clear round that is always the aim of the rider who goes first. The nervous tension disappeared as Malcolm sent me on my way with that wonderful boost to my confidence.

I reached the steeplechase course to find a hot-air balloon, with people aboard, drifting no more than 50 feet above the start – it was the last thing I needed. The energetic Malcolm was beside me as the starter began jabbering in a totally incomprehensible language (unless you happen to speak Danish, which I assume it was) at the end of which he said, 'Go.'

I dithered, not knowing whether this really was my signal to start. Malcolm, equally confused, asked, 'Do you mean she has to go *now*?'

'Go . . . go,' said the starter, while the clock was already ticking away.

I must have lost about ten seconds before I set off into the fog on the steeplechase course, but Priceless managed to finish less than a second over the optimum time for just 0.8 of a penalty. I had been in an agony of indecision over the route I would take at one of the cross-country fences, the Horsens Bridge, until deciding that I would wait and see how P jumped the water on the steeplechase. If he jumped it from a long way back, I wouldn't risk the fast and direct route at the Horsens Bridge; an early take-off there would almost certainly land us in a crumpled heap in the ditch on the landing side. Priceless gave me the clear-cut answer I needed by standing way back at the steeplechase water both times he jumped it. I would definitely take the slower alternative at the Bridge. It's amazing how one reaches these decisions.

When I completed the steeplechase I discovered that P had lost a hind shoe. There should have been a farrier there to put a new shoe on him, but he was caught up in the crowds and hadn't yet arrived, so I had no alternative but to press ahead, picking the best ground I could on the second section of the roads and tracks in the hope that his foot wouldn't be damaged. I can remember battling my way through amazingly large crowds shouting excuse me in as many languages as I could muster. A farrier was waiting for us when we reached the Box for the ten-minute halt, which felt more like ten seconds, before I was venturing forth on the re-shod Priceless to tackle those alarming cross-country fences.

The double of post and rails at number eight had worried me. There was a drop down on to the road after the first element, then you had to bounce straight over the second part which had another drop down into a field. I have never liked bounces; I'm always much happier when the horse has room for a stride between the two parts of a double. In this case, both fences were at maximum height and I had thought they looked enormous when I inspected them on foot.

Priceless, however, made it feel wonderfully easy. He is a brilliant horse to ride across country and I can't pretend that I contributed much to his clear round, except to point him in the right direction. I had finished soon after 10 a.m. and spent the rest of the day either waiting for the other British riders as they came into the Box, or rushing round to watch them. All of them jumped clear rounds, except poor Lizzie Purbrick, who went really well but had an unlucky fall at the water. Rachel Bayliss probably missed her chance of an individual medal when Mystic Minstrel lost a shoe on the first section of roads and tracks and she was forced to go much faster than she would have wished in order to leave time for it to be nailed on before the steeplechase.

Meanwhile our team was in the lead and we were in high spirits when we returned to the agricultural college that evening for dinner.

77

The room had been laid out with a table for each team, on which stood a jug of water and a chocolate cake. We took our places with more or less perfect decorum, and I was in the middle of telling a story when a Frenchman came up behind me and tipped a full jug of cold water straight over my head.

'Hang on a minute,' I said, as I stood up and turned to face him, whereupon a chocolate cake was neatly planted in my face. I couldn't see or speak, I could scarcely breathe.

Sue Benson promptly stood up and said, 'How dare you be so unbearable to my friend,' while she pushed a chocolate cake into his face. Richard Meade then leapt into the fray, armed with more chocolate cakes, and pandemonium ensued. Everyone in the room entered into this incredible water and chocolate cake battle, which went on for about an hour and left the room that had been so carefully prepared for us a scene of total devastation.

Eventually some semblance of adulthood and responsibility returned. We then set about clearing up the terrible mess we had made. It took us a couple of hours and we thought we made a pretty good job of it. But the British were blamed for the fiasco and we were told the following morning that we would not be allowed to have any breakfast, even though the French were tucking in. Malcolm Wallace, who had been at a chefs d'équipe function that evening, did his best to defend us (not quite believing his ears on hearing the story), but I think we may still have been reported to the international federation for the bad behaviour which was blamed entirely on the British. I can't think how the French got away with it.

We didn't go hungry that morning. Fred's Cafe had nothing on the caravan, where my mother and Dot handed out bacon and eggs to an army of starving riders. Nor did we lose our cool by throwing away the team title that was already within our grasp. None of the British riders achieved an individual medal, but we won the team gold, which we regarded as the most important of all. Switzerland's Hansueli Schmutz won the individual title on Oran while we took some of the minor awards: I was sixth, Richard Meade seventh, Tiny Clapham eighth and Rachel Bayliss eleventh.

I returned home in time to grab a few clean clothes before setting out for Burghley, which began a few days later. Lucinda Prior-Palmer won there on Beagle Bay, with Richard Meade second on Speculator III, while I was third on Night Cap. I hoped that the British National Insurance Group would now appreciate that there were two really good young horses in the Holgate stable!

A date was made to arrange details of the sponsorship deal at which my Uncle Jack, who is joint-owner of both Priceless and Night Cap, would be present. He has looked after all the financial affairs for my mother and myself since we lost my father, and he administrates a small family trust of which Mummy and I are both directors. Uncle Jack has been an important part of my life since those early days at school when he collected me for weekends, giving me the wonderful chance to enjoy all the home comforts provided by his wife, who has since, alas, died. He used to watch me riding at Benenden, and it was he who insisted I should be given a chance to continue with horses, because he believed I showed some talent.

My mother suggests this might not have been the only reason why I was given the opportunity. 'Your Uncle Jack thinks you can do nothing wrong,' she says, 'so I always take anything he says about you with a pinch of salt.'

I personally don't think *he* can do much wrong either. He has given me marvellous support over the years and has rarely missed any important event in which I'm competing. Though few people realised it, he nobly supported the Holgate eventing team with its overdrafts, tears and occasional successes, for nearly ten years. Now he felt tremendous relief at the thought that his bank balance would at last become healthier thanks to a company sponsor.

I was obviously glad to know that he would be there, using his astute brain, when the sponsorship details were worked out with Gordon Miller. Before the meeting it had occurred to me that the lorry we were using to take the horses to events was at death's door. I urgently needed a new one, but who would pay for it? I kept those thoughts to myself until half-way through the meeting, when I had the awful cheek to say, 'I'm terribly sorry about this, Mr Miller, but I'm not sure that we can accept your kind offer unless you are able to supply us with a horsebox, because the one we're using now is dying.'

Uncle Jack nearly fell off his chair and Mr Miller choked in his tea. I pretended to remain cool as a cucumber, although I was actually sweating profusely.

'I expect we can manage that,' said Gordon Miller, as he recovered – at which I only just managed to refrain from plastering him with kisses.

It was agreed that the American-owned British National Insurance Group would pay for the cost of three horses – Priceless, Night Cap and a five-year-old newcomer to our stables called Riotous – for a period of three years from November 1981. They also replaced our ailing lorry with a marvellous smart new vehicle which had my sponsor's name on both sides. We aptly named her the Queen Mary.

Despite the initial hassle with the fat bald men at the Inn on the Park, I couldn't have been luckier. My sponsors were enthusiastic, supportive and incredibly understanding. The feeling of gratitude, which began with the signing of that initial contract in 1981, was to increase as I realised my great good fortune during the years that followed.

In December of 1981, while Lucinda Prior-Palmer was marrying David Green, I was in New Zealand with Mark Todd. I had spoken to Mark for the first time at Brigstock in 1980 and had wondered what on earth this unknown Kiwi was doing in England. To my surprise, he said that he had come over to compete at Badminton.

To everyone's surprise, including mine, he went on to win the 1980 Badminton Championship on a horse called Southern Comfort. After watching his victory on television, I sent him a funny poem that said well done to the Kiwi on his great win, etc. I had thought he would be returning home for good afterwards, instead of which he came to live at Great Somerford in Wiltshire, which was quite close to us after we had moved to Ivyleaze.

By then Philip Moseby and I were (and still are) 'just good friends'. Toddy and I had started going out together before I made the trip to New Zealand, where his parents and grandparents (known as 'Pop' and 'Mumma') were wonderfully hospitable. I stayed with his parents at their lovely house in Cambridge when I wasn't travelling around giving lessons at the pre-arranged clinics, which gave me a chance to see the country and helped to pay for my fare from home.

During that trip, Toddy told me that he was going to break in some three-year-old horses on Pop's farm just outside Cambridge. So I went with him one morning and, to my amazement, he lassoed one of these youngsters, tied it to a tree with a special knot and then said that it was time for us to go and have some coffee. By the time we returned, the horse had pulled back at the tree a few times and was considered halter-broken. Toddy led it along and it was as quiet as a lamb.

The next stage was to put the saddle on and lunge the youngster with one leg tied up, which was to teach it not to buck when saddled.

'It's barbaric,' I said, after watching the horse being lunged on three legs. Apparently it was common practice in New Zealand to tie each leg up in turn and lunge any unbroken youngsters in this way; then, if it started playing up on four legs, one would be tied up again. As

Toddy pointed out, there was no resistance to this method; the horse actually lifted his leg up waiting for it to be tied. I can't say that I have been tempted to try the method myself, but I had to admit that this particular three-year-old seemed totally unperturbed.

By then Toddy had sold his Badminton winner, Southern Comfort, to Torrance Watkins-Fleischmann in America. He therefore had no horse to ride at Badminton, and as a result, no reason for returning to England. After a marvellous trip, which lasted several months, I came home on my own to prepare for my first season as a sponsored rider.

EIGHT

World Championships

Priceless gave me a fantastic ride across country at Badminton in 1982 and he finished within the optimum time, which I regarded as a significant feather in his cap. He is not a particularly fast horse, but he can gallop and jump in rhythm which, in my book, is far more important. People are still inclined to believe that you need a wonderful racehorse to get inside the time, though I believe Priceless has already proved that to be nonsense.

Richard Meade won the Whitbread Trophy at Badminton that year, from America's Bruce Davidson (who was then the reigning World Champion) and Rachel Bayliss. I was fourth on Priceless and felt on top of the world; the horse had given me great confidence and we were obviously now in line for a place on the World Championships team that would be competing at Luhmühlen in Germany in the autumn.

My place was confirmed after P won the final trial, again staged at the Midland Bank Championships in Locko Park, and my mood would still have been buoyant if I hadn't taken a crashing fall with Riotous on the same day, for which I felt I was entirely to blame.

We had bought Riotous (another horse by Ben Faerie) as a five-year-old and he had already done a couple of events with his previous owner. He had the ability to jump fences that I regarded as very big – such as a 4 feet 10 inch square parallel in the school at home – but he found it difficult to stand off at them. If I dared him on a long stride, he would suddenly shorten, put in an extra one and jump from the base of the obstacle. I found this slightly unnerving, but thought it was probably because he had evented before and that I could get him out of it.

I took him to Locko because he had qualified for the Novice Championship and we came unstuck at one of the angled fences, where he veered off a straight line and landed too close to the second element, where he turned a somersault. I always hate to leave a horse on a bad note and therefore decided that I would take Riotous to Rotherfield, to give him one more competition – and, I hoped, erase his unpleasant memory of Locko – before I went to the World Championships.

The evening before Rotherfield, a Swiss event rider called Roland Straub arrived for supper. By now Mark Todd was one of my best friends and Roland was the man of the moment. We sat and talked until a ridiculously late hour and, after he had left, we were horrified to learn that he had had a crash on his way back to stay with Tomi Gretener, another Swiss event rider, who was living near Cheltenham.

Fortunately no one was badly hurt, but my mother and I were both feeling very upset and she said it would be daft for me to compete at Rotherfield after such a trauma.

'It's no good telling me that because I've got to go there,' I replied, stubbornly. So Louise Bates, who was staying with us, set off with me the following morning, both of us fairly bleary-eyed.

Towards the end of the Rotherfield cross-country course there were some upright park rails into the woods, where you then had to turn to jump the water. I can remember coming down the hill towards the park rails and thinking: this is a fence that I'm really going to respect, I'm going to be absolutely accurate. I steadied Riotous and set him up so that he could take it as he would a show jump, but he failed to make the height and we had another crashing fall. This time he landed on top of me and, for a few unnerving moments, I was pinned to the ground. Eventually, he clambered to his feet and I remounted to finish the course.

My confidence was now in shreds after those two falls with Riotous.

'What *did* I do wrong?' I asked David Green, who had been standing beside the park rails when I fell at Rotherfield.

'You did nothing wrong,' he said. 'The horse obviously saw the darkness in the woods on the other side of the fence and didn't pick up.'

But that wasn't enough reassurance for me. I went off to Wylye for the final training before the World Championships feeling thoroughly undermined.

Lady Hugh, who could see that I was in a right old state when I arrived at Wylye, decided it was essential to get me into a better frame of mind.

'We'll get Night Cap out, as he's not going to the World Championships,' she said. 'We'll go up to the top and you can jump ten cross-country fences on him, then you'll be fine.'

I rode poor Mr N so appallingly badly that Lady Hugh stopped me before we fell flat on our faces. Night Cap had so far managed to stay on his feet, while I seemed to be doing my best to bring him down.

'It's no good, Lady Hugh, I don't know how to ride any more,' I said, tearfully.

'We'll have to get Priceless,' she told my mother, who went off to fetch P from his stable.

Whereas Night Cap tends to listen to his rider and can therefore find himself in trouble if the signals are faulty, Priceless works everything out for himself. He totally ignored all the wrong moves I made at Wylye that day and went sailing over ten of the cross-country fences to restore my shattered confidence. Even so, I arrived in Luhmühlen feeling that I was ill-prepared for a major three-day event. Thank goodness Dot and my mother were there to sharpen me up.

There was always a temptation during the final training sessions at Wylye to do too much, to feel you had to take advantage of the superb facilities and iron out all the weak spots, whether real or imaginary. I can remember Richard Meade saying to me before we left for the World Championships, 'Don't do anything more than you would normally do at home.' He was quite right; I was tending to overdo the training without realising it.

I can honestly say that I have always wanted to be a good team member above all else. But it isn't always easy during the final build-up to international championships, when nerves are a little frayed, to appreciate how others are coping with the tension. If one rider seems upset and another appears to be cruelly indifferent, rather than consoling, it may mean that they are both feeling equally nervous and are reacting to it in different ways.

It was quite difficult for me to know how to transmit my own sense of team spirit before Luhmühlen. I was the whipper-snapper, riding on the team with Rachel Bayliss and two of the world's leading riders, Lucinda Green and Richard Meade. Clissy Strachan, my former instructor, and Tiny Clapham were competing as individuals. I wanted to be known as an up-and-coming rider, who was also a good team member, rather than a cocky little upstart who didn't know when to keep her mouth shut. I doubt whether I managed to get the balance right, but I did my best!

As in Horsens the previous year, Malcolm Wallace asked me to go first for the team and I was happy to comply. I had gone first once before and it had worked well; with both Lucinda and Richard there, it was obviously right for the team that they should have the last two places. It meant that my own slim chance of winning an individual medal was reduced; apart from the need for the first rider to go steadily and safely across country, it's a well-known fact that subconsciously the dressage judges tend to be a little more severe on those who go early.

But we were there as a team and, at the risk of sounding boring and pompous, I don't believe you deserve to ride for your country if you only care about your own self-interest. You certainly don't deserve to win a team medal unless you are prepared to contribute some help to your fellow riders. I didn't do anything noble in Luhmühlen, where I was far too inexperienced to be considered for Lucinda's third place, or for Richard's even more responsible fourth place as the final team member. But I'm convinced that we need to work together, as unselfishly as we can, when we are lucky enough to be chosen to ride for Britain, whether as a junior, a young rider or a senior.

I have to admit I again felt a little harshly treated by the dressage judges when my score was announced in Luhmühlen, but that was far easier to shrug aside than the habitual gnawing anxiety regarding my own ability after I have made a mistake. In any case there's no time to harp back to dressage scores when cross-country day is near at hand. That needs all your concentration.

Having inspected the course in detail, Malcolm Wallace made sure that we were familiar with all the possible alternatives at each of the thirty-two cross-country fences. As was his normal practice he arranged a meeting for all the British riders, which was held on the Thursday evening. By then we had walked the course at least a couple of times and the purpose of this get-together was to discuss, with the help of drawings prepared by Eddie Farmer, how we planned to jump.

'Right, Ginny,' Wol might say, 'where are you going to take fence one?'

So I'd tell him which way I intended to go and the others would do the same. We'd discuss every fence in this way, with all the different alternatives, so that we all knew which way everyone else planned to go. If a problem was mentioned that we hadn't noticed, we still had time to go back and inspect the fence in the light of this new knowledge the following day. Routes A, B and C were so firmly implanted in our minds that we could switch plans if the chosen route seemed to be riding badly on the actual day. If, for instance, I reported back to Wol at the end of my cross-country that I'd had a hiccup on route A at fence four, that it wasn't riding as well as we'd hoped, he would be able to tell the others, 'Route B is now in action at fence four.'

We all had tremendous respect for our chef d'équipe and his careful attention to detail. What is more, he was also a great friend – which is a very rare combination – and I think we were all prepared to jump our guts out for him. I know that I always felt marvellous if, at the end of my round, I did well enough for him to pat me on the shoulder and say, 'Well done, Bloodshot.' The name was given to me in Luhmühlen, due to my appearance each morning after I had made the early struggle out of bed.

After the two days of dressage, Rachel Bayliss and Mystic Minstrel were in the lead, as they had been in Horsens, while there was scarcely anything to choose between the top three teams – the Germans, Americans and ourselves. We knew that the long cross-country course was going to be tiring and that it was likely to sort us all out. My instructions were to jump a safe clear round.

Thanks to Priceless, who again jumped beautifully, we finished clear with just 8.8 time penalties. It was then my job to pass on any relevant information. I felt (and still do) that it's essential to be correct and honest at this stage; if you do have a near-miss at one particular fence, you have to swallow your pride and say, 'I was very lucky.'

On that occasion, I had a slight problem at the first water complex (fence six) and I remember saying, 'You have to kick on much more than I thought at the island fence in the middle, because Priceless really had to stretch for it.'

Sadly, Rachel Bayliss had a stop there with Mystic Minstrel and – because the Germans and Americans were still looking threatening – Malcolm's instructions to both Lucinda on Regal Realm and Richard on Kilcashel were to go clear, *within* the time. It seemed like a tall order, but they both showed their true colours by doing exactly as Wol had asked. Thanks to those two, we were marginally in the lead at the end of the day.

There had been a tragic accident during the cross-country. The Swiss rider Ernest Baumann was killed when his horse, Beaujour de Mars, somersaulted on to him at the second water complex towards the end of the course. Malcolm told each one of us this awful news after we had completed the course; he reckoned that it should be kept from anyone who was still waiting to ride across country. I didn't know the rider, but it was still a dreadful shock and our hearts went out to his family and his fellow Swiss riders, who all withdrew after hearing the news of their friend's death.

Apart from that tragedy, it was a marvellous event and no script writer could have contrived a more nail-biting finale. Our team was just over 1 point ahead of the United States, with Germany less than a point behind them. Lucinda was lying second for the individual title, marginally over the cost of one show jumping error behind Germany's Helmut Rethemeier on Santiago.

After Priceless had jumped a clear round, I clambered on to the crowded back of Lady Hugh's famous mini-moke to watch the contest as it reached its climax. We cheered ecstatically when Lucinda went clear on Regal Realm, strengthening our chances of the team gold medal and ensuring that she would win the individual silver – or even, though it seemed unlikely, the gold. About a dozen of us were perilously perched on the mini-moke when Helmut Rethemeier came in, knowing that he could only make one error if he were to win the individual championship. He hit two parts of the treble and, in the thrilling realisation that Lucinda had won, we all lost our balance on the mini-moke and tumbled out on to the wet grass.

Richard's round, so crucial to the team, was still to come. We now had two fences in hand for the team gold, but we still watched with our hearts in our mouths until Richard rode through the finish on Kilcashel, having made only one mistake, giving us victory over Germany and the United States.

A double gold is a fine excuse for a big celebration. There were no jugs of water or chocolate cakes for our huge party in the stables that evening; we made do with the vast quantities of champagne that Malcolm Wallace had rushed off to buy! We had finished with five riders in the top ten – Lucinda Green (first), Richard Meade (fifth), Clissy Strachan (sixth), myself (seventh) and Tiny Clapham (tenth). We were not going to let that moment of glory go by without dragging in all our friends – the other riders, grooms, the press and anyone else we happened to spot – to join us in the celebrations.

Lord Hugh Russell made his own spectacular contribution to that wonderful evening. For a laugh, Lucinda had bought him a pair of Union Jack underpants and told him to remember which team he was supporting. While we were celebrating in style, Lord Hugh suddenly appeared on a bicycle, with an umbrella over his head and wearing only his red, white and blue underpants. He was greeted with a great roar of laughter and approval.

That same evening, Tiny Clapham and I had decided (quite wrongly as it turned out) that the Danish rider, Nils Haagensen, lacked a sense of humour and we subjected him to endless teasing. He had proved his talent as an event rider when winning the 1979 European Championships and the 1980 'Substitute' Olympic Three-Day Event, but we weren't giving too much heed to his record as we played our ridiculous pranks on him – like tying a stock round his neck in a bow and putting flowers in his hair so he looked like the pet of the Chelsea Flower Show. We were somewhat surprised to realise that he found it all terribly funny! He then thought we were a bit wimpish when we declined the offer to dance with him on the rather frail tables. We had no regrets as we watched him gracefully disappear through the centre of one.

The other abiding memory of that evening was the feeling of pride in Lucinda's marvellous victory. I can remember wondering – without a trace of envy – how I would have felt if I had just become the World Champion, and how she must feel now. As far as I was concerned there was no one who deserved it more. I had been studying her on video for the last few years – not to copy her, because I don't think that's possible, but to try and pin-point why she was so brilliant across country. Her rhythm and position had always seemed flawless.

I used to play her from take-off to landing in slow motion, watching her position, noting that she was never in front of the horse's movement coming into a fence. If the horse did make a mistake, she was therefore never in a position to lose her balance as it was trying to get out of trouble. Her hips were down and her shoulders forward, so that she was going with the horse's movement but was still ready to cope with any problem.

It was also obvious from my video viewing that Lucinda's reactions were razor sharp. If in trouble, her legs would instantly shoot forward, putting her in the perfect position to stay on board, whatever happened. I have never seen her fall off. I've only seen her have a fall with a horse – as, for instance, when Be Fair turned over at the crooked S at Badminton way back in 1974, when I was having my first ride there on Dubonnet.

The thing that stuck most in my mind after watching Lucinda on video was that I must learn to ride with my hips down – not on the horse's back, but near it. I had to keep my shoulders forward and go with the movement, but not in front of it, otherwise I would then topple straight over the horse's head if it stopped or blundered. It was easier to reach this conclusion than to put it into practice.

Three days after that incredible party in Luhmühlen, I was walking the course at Burghley. I was to partner Night Cap over the Lincolnshire cross-country fences exactly one week after taking

Priceless on the long haul round Luhmühlen and I had another good ride. At last I felt all our past moments of misunderstanding each other were behind us. It was marred the following day when I slipped from third to fifth with two mistakes in the show jumping. This comparatively insignificant taste of Herr Rethemeier's medicine was a sharp reminder of what the German must have felt a week earlier as we fell out of the mini-moke in a joyous heap.

Later that year we very nearly lost Priceless. He had taken part in the parade of medallists at Olympia and, back at home the following day, it was obvious that something was wrong with him. We stayed up with him all through the next night, worried sick about his condition, and in the morning my mother phoned Don Attenburrow in Devon. Although we had moved, Don was (and still is) the person to whom we instantly turned for veterinary help.

Blood samples were taken, but we were watching Priceless deteriorate as we waited for the results to come through. He was very jaundiced – 'as yellow as a lemon' as Don puts it, and he stood in his stable with head down, slightly rocking and visibly losing weight. At one stage we tried to put him in the lorry to take him down to Don's place near Exeter. He was in a muck sweat after walking across the yard and, when we got him into the lorry, he was blowing as much as if he'd been round a cross-country course. It was obvious that he was too ill to make the journey, so he stayed at home.

It's entirely thanks to Don Attenburrow that Priceless is still alive. He diagnosed the condition as leptospirosis, a bacterial infection that is usually carried in mouse or rat excreta, and he treated it accordingly. Priceless had presumably eaten some hay on which an infected rodent had urinated.

Don prescribed antibiotics and glucose. He said that Priceless's condition would have to be monitored with two-hourly checks on his temperature, pulse and respiration. We organised a twenty-four-hour rota; I would do the midnight and 2 a.m. shifts, with someone else taking over for the next two – and so on.

For about six weeks we recorded all the information from these two-hourly checks and we were all totally exhausted at the end but, thank God, we saved him. My world would have fallen apart if we had lost this tough, down-to-earth bloke, with his small piggy eyes and habit of greeting me in the stable with an aggressive ears-laid-back expression. The welcome is a little more civil if I take some horse nuts with me, but he doesn't share Mr N's taste for polo mints – they're much too high-class for him.

It was while Priceless was ill that I bought a horse on my own, without either my mother or Dot present, for the first time in my life. I was feeling very low because of P's condition and not at all in the right frame of mind for the cocktail party in Sussex which my sponsors had asked me to attend. The horse was advertised in *Horse and Hound* as a four-year-old strawberry roan and, since I would be passing the owner's place on the way to the party, I decided that I might as well take a look.

I liked Murphy Himself's dark grey head (in fact he's mostly grey, with some bay hairs), but it was seeing him trot that really excited me because he has such wonderful movement. Doing my best to retain a non-committal expression, I watched while he was ridden towards some cross poles. He ran out at them three times. This horse is quite a character, I thought, as the embarrassed owner tried to explain that Murphy had never, ever run out before. After that he jumped some quite big fences – indeed I was a bit horrified by the size of them, considering he was only a four-year-old – but there was no doubt that this horse, with his super action, was also able to jump.

'I'll have him subject to the vet's examination,' I said, secretly praying that my mother would like him.

When I rang home to tell her, my mother was surprised and speechless. However, after Murphy had been delivered to us, both she and Dot decided he was lovely, so all was well. The only serious doubts we have ever had about him concern his age. When we bought him Don Attenburrow was not totally convinced that he was a four-year-old, but said that he could be, so we went along with the idea that the age on his papers was correct. The doubts crept in during 1985 when he was, supposedly, a seven-year-old – with a set of six-year-old teeth!

NINE

Frauenfeld and Burghley

While Priceless was fighting for his life, Night Cap began his three-month training programme for Badminton, starting with three weeks of walking on the roads to strengthen his slack muscles. There was no way that P, hoping that he did survive, would be ready to go to Badminton or to the European Championships in Switzerland that summer and we obviously passed this information on to the selectors.

I was naturally hoping that they would be impressed with Mr N when they saw him competing at Badminton and was terribly disappointed when he had a stop coming out of the quarry. It was entirely due to my bad riding; I had over-ridden him at the wall going into the quarry, where he jumped far too big, and he was hopelessly unbalanced for the steps coming out. Having clambered up them, he stopped at the rails on top for an expensive 20 penalties. Lucinda Green won on Regal Realm with another brilliant round across country and I was eleventh on Night Cap. Needless to say, Lucinda was included on the 'long-list' for the European Championships which was announced immediately after Badminton – and, thankfully, so was I.

Shortly afterwards I flew to New Zealand, where I had been invited to ride a borrowed horse in two events. It was hoped that I would help to promote the sport and give an extra fillip to the various functions that were being organised to raise funds for the Olympic team. Little did anyone realise that the result in Los Angeles was to make the sport famous all over New Zealand.

Mark Todd was then riding a smashing new horse, Fran Clark's Charisma. He would certainly have belonged to anyone's list of 'horses to watch', but you would hardly have tipped him as the future Olympic gold medallist, even though he won both the events in which I rode. The first was a one-day event at Clevedon, near Auckland and I had just two days to get acquainted with Mrs Anderson's part-bred Arab, Casino, before the contest began. We had one cross-country refusal to drop out of contention and another at the Taupo Three-Day, where

Casino was leading the intermediate section after the dressage and would have won but for that single stop at one of the easiest fences. I was getting a bit tired of those single refusals that seemed to be dogging my life in eventing since Night Cap was penalised at Badminton.

I have always loved flying, but I lost my taste for it for a while after the journey home from New Zealand. As we landed, the plane went out of control and people screamed as it swerved to left and right up the runway, first on one wheel and then on the other. I clutched some poor unsuspecting gentleman on my left and refused to let him go, much to his astonishment. I thought my hour had come as the pilot fought to bring his huge Jumbo under control and eventually succeeded. We were all white and shaking by the time we left the plane. I always thought I'd be brave on such an occasion – how wrong I was!

Despite the hiccup at Badminton, and much to my delight, Night Cap and I were chosen for the European Championships team. At that stage I was worried because I had nowhere suitable to gallop the horses and I mentioned this to Mimi May, with whom Mark Todd was then staying. She nobly said that she would ask whether I could use Jeremy Tree's gallops, near Marlborough, and word came back that the trainer had very kindly agreed. When I saw his gallops, I thought I was looking at paradise.

There was a wonderful all-weather 7-furlong gallop and, unlike the flat land around home, surrounding hills that you could trot up and down if you wished. These are always helpful when you are building up a horse's muscles before a three-day event. Since then I have regularly used Jeremy Tree's gallops, obviously at times which fit in with his training schedules, and it has been a tremendous advantage – apart from which the horses love it. It takes forty-five minutes to drive there, but you couldn't think of a more worthwhile journey.

There was more valuable help from the National Hunt world when I studied and discussed the methods used to train steeplechasers and hurdlers to the required fitness. During the comparatively quiet summer months after my return from New Zealand, I acquired an entirely new schedule that I planned to use on my event horses. I had not been entirely satisfied with their fitness using my own method of training and it was thanks to my National Hunt friends that I discovered a quite different approach that has been wonderfully effective.

It was too late to introduce new ideas into Night Cap's preparation for the European Championships, but he did have the benefit of working on Jeremy Tree's gallops before I took him to Wylye for our final training. Anxious, as always, about the thoroughness of our preparations, I suddenly decided that N needed to go and paddle in a river, that it was an essential part of getting him ready for whatever jumps into water they had designed for us in Frauenfeld. He had not, I told myself, jumped into water recently so it really seemed a matter of some urgency. I therefore rode him into a stretch of river which we had previously used at Wylye and he paddled around happily enough; there was nothing to suggest that he had developed a sudden aversion to water. But I was still not content.

Finding another section of the river, which had beautiful shingle and looked fantastic, I decided we must have another paddle. So I rode him down the bank and into the water, without checking it first, and he sank down to his knees. He had a terrifying struggle to extricate himself and, when I had eventually dragged him out to safety, I burst into tears. He might easily have pulled a muscle as he floundered in the mud.

I was in a terrible state when I phoned Louise Bates, then Dot and my mother, before I even dared to confess my stupidity to Lady Hugh.

'You're a twit,' she told me, as if I didn't know already. 'No one has ever gone into that part of the river.'

Night Cap seemed to be none the worse for his adventure, so Lady Hugh suggested we should take him to the dew pond fence at Wylye just to make sure, for my sake more than anyone else's, that he was still willing to jump into water. He popped in without a moment's hesitation and that should have been enough to convince me all was well.

Two British horses had to be withdrawn from the European Championships through last-minute lameness – Richard Meade's Kilcashel and Mike Tucker's super home-bred General Bugle, who had finished second at Badminton earlier that year. I therefore took the place which Richard Meade had occupied in the World Championships and went last for the team, with Tiny Clapham first, followed by Lorna Clarke and Lucinda Green. Rachel Bayliss was our only individual rider.

But it was Malcolm Wallace who produced the first spectacular British feat. We had been invited to a dinner high up in the hills at a former monastery on the day before the Championships began and, when our superb meal was over, the pranks began. A Swiss rider performed a dangerous somersault over a chair that had been placed on a narrow turret wall, with a sheer drop below it. This startling acrobatic feat was followed by a bet that no one else could do it. Since the Brits have always been competitors, I immediately volunteered our poor chef d'équipe! While Mrs Wol looked on in horror, our man executed a perfect somersault over the chair and landed safely to deafening cheers. The problems we were to face on the cross-country course seemed tame in comparison.

This time I had the advantage of all the information that our earlier riders were bringing back to the Box. Tiny Clapham and Windjammer were among those who fell at the water, which was part of the twenty-eighth fence, with only one more to jump before the finish. The water was fairly deep and those who went in fast were tending to lose their feet and take a ducking. Our second team rider, Lorna Clarke, had also fallen during a bold round on Danville, before Lucinda whizzed through clear in her customary style on Regal Realm. Tiny and Lorna had remounted to finish, but they had both incurred 60 penalties for a fall. If our team were to have a chance of retaining the European title, I needed to follow Lucinda's example with a fast clear round.

It was desperately hot, with the temperature high in the eighties, and it didn't help when Night Cap twice lost a shoe, first on the steeplechase and then on the cross-country. But all was still well as I came into the water at fence twenty-eight. Lucinda had told me that I must ride into it slowly, on a very short and bouncy stride, that if I went in fast I'd be bound to have a fall. The aim was to pop over the barrels, take a couple of short strides on dry land and splash gently through the deep water.

Like an idiot I over-checked, lost all my forward impulsion, and Night Cap came to a grinding half in front of the barrels. I could have killed myself for those 20 totally unnecessary penalties for a refusal. Mr N is the sort of horse you can stop with one tug; had I ridden him in stronger, I could easily have brought him back to a virtual halt as he landed. Later, as I agonised over it a thousand times on video, I realised that the earlier mishap in the river at Wylye had still been rankling. The psychological scar it had left, the fear that Night Cap might now have an aversion to water, had affected the way I had ridden. It wasn't the horse who had stopped; it was the rider.

We were second of the eleven teams at the end of the cross-country, fairly close behind Sweden, with France a long way back in third place. Our individual rider Rachel Bayliss was leading after a marvellous performance on Mystic Minstrel. We were thrilled for her when she won the title and for Lucinda when she moved up from third to win the individual silver.

Night Cap finished eighth, and we took the team silver medals. We had finished 11.7 penalties behind the winning Swedish team, even though Tiny and Lorna had their falls and I had my refusal.

'Tell me the truth,' I said to Dot, before we left for home. 'What did I do wrong at that cross-country fence?'

'You rode in too slowly,' she said, giving me the honest answer that I'd asked for, 'never mind, eh.' This last phrase has been used on many occasions by Dot, always with a huge smile. There are obstacles that we call 'never-mind-eh fences' and now Dot has a sweater with the inscription on it. But it may already have become evident that I am not particularly good at taking that sort of advice.

I hope that this self-destructive remorse was not too evident as we drank champagne in the stables after the medals had been presented – and as Rachel was thrown in the water trough in recognition of her individual victory. We went out for a lovely meal that evening with my friend Roland Straub and with Reto Straub (not a relation), who was president of the veterinary committee in Frauenfeld. The Swedish riders were there and we drank toasts to the new team champions and to Rachel, our individual heroine, with Lorna Clarke reeling off an amazingly long repertoire of jokes.

Rachel was going to be at a loose end after we flew back to England and were waiting for the horses to arrive, so I persuaded her to come home with me. Louise joined us and we raved it up for several days, celebrating the success of our new European Champion in some style.

After our final late night out, we crawled into our beds looking forward to a long and undisturbed sleep. We were to be awoken abruptly at 6 a.m. with a violent pounding on the door. 'Ginny, wake up and come quickly,' called an urgent voice.

I leapt out of bed, thinking the house was on fire or the horses had escaped, to learn that every single piece of tack we owned had been stolen – some £4,000 worth. The burglars' haul included seven saddles and ten bridles; rugs, headcollars, lungeing reins and all our other equipment had gone. After much Sherlock Holmes detective work from our local policeman and myself, it was discovered that the burglars had the gall to use *our* wheelbarrow to ferry the tack to a waiting car. While Louise, Rachel and I were sleeping peacefully, they must have made a number of journeys wheeling the stolen goods through the yard, across the arena and down through the fields to the getaway vehicle. We were all furious at having slept so soundly.

We were to pick up my mother and Dorothy from Wylye later that day and I dreaded having to tell them about the theft. They were both exhausted after the long journey home from Frauenfeld with the horses, and the news I had to impart to them was not exactly cheering. Since then our security has gone over board. In addition to our alarm systems, we have two monster Rottweilers to act as guard dogs. Let them try again!

Meanwhile Priceless, now fully recovered from his illness, was getting fit for Burghley. I was not in the best frame of mind to do him justice, I felt that I couldn't seem to get it together and was convinced that my wonderful horses would do much better with another jockey. As on previous occasions, I did some soul-searching with my mother, Pat Burgess and Dot.

Now that she knows me well, Lucinda is also good at prodding me in the right direction. If necessary, she'll tell me to stop feeling sorry for myself — which is a real, effective dig in the heart. On other occasions, she can giggle me out of my gloom. I hope that I've learnt enough from her to give some encouragement, in my turn, to other people when they're feeling low.

Thanks to the Good Lord and to Priceless, the gloom that followed Frauenfeld was dispersed a few weeks later at Burghley. P was in the lead at the end of the dressage, so we had made a good start; but the cross-country problems were still to be solved, especially those posed by a new fence called the Brandy Glass. I must have spent about four hours looking at it from every angle.

The quick way was to bounce through the middle, but I had decided I didn't much like that route long before Australia's Helen Carr (who was the second to go) attempted it and fell with Champagne Charlie. There was an almost equally quick way if you jumped two rails at an angle, followed by a V-shaped corner. If any horse can jump that route it's Priceless, I told myself, as i studied the fence.

I had reached this conclusion when America's Bruce Davidson, who was also studying the various alternatives, asked me how I planned to jump it. 'On the left,' I said, referring to that line across the two rails and the corner.

Bruce came across me on the Friday evening when I was walking my route B, the bounce through the middle. 'I might have known that you had a different plan,' he said, tapping me on the shoulder.

'You're so wrong,' I told him, incensed by the implication that I had been less than honest. 'I intend to take the left route.'

'Seeing is believing,' said Bruce, with a knowing smile.

Shortly before I set out on the cross-country, Malcolm Wallace and Louise Bates rushed over to the Box to tell me that they had been watching the closed-circuit television, and had timed the people before me. If I landed over the Flight Butt in eight minutes, I could take the slow and circuitous route through the Brandy Glass and still finish within the optimum time. When I reached that spot, my stop-watch showed me that it had taken me eight minutes exactly; from there to the Brandy Glass, which was a fairly long gallop, I was saying to myself, will I – won't I – will I – won't I? Priceless was giving me a wonderful ride and I had walked the fast route so many times that I knew it much better than the slower alternative. I also had something I wanted to prove to Bruce Davidson! On the other hand, Louise and Wol would kill me if I went the fast way and made a mess of it. What should I do?

As I came round a bend towards the fence, I found myself on line for the quick two rails and corner. Blow it, I thought, I'll go straight on. Once committed, I was petrified of making a mistake, but he jumped it brilliantly. In my delight and relief, I gave P a big pat on the neck; he hates being patted and he put his ears flat back as he galloped on.

Having finished about twenty seconds within the time, I found Louise and Wol shaking their fists at me. 'How could you do that to us?' they demanded. They had both been watching the closed-circuit television and Wol had informed everyone within earshot that I was going to take the long route at the Brandy Glass. Apparently his head bobbed up and down three times in disbelief as Priceless made his three jumps through the fast route.

'If it had been a team event, you know I would have done as I was told,' I said to Wol, in answer to his teasing reprimands about the embarrassment I'd caused him. Bruce Davidson was nice enough to say that he wouldn't misunderstand me in the future!

My mother had also been watching me on closed-circuit television and, not knowing who she was, the people around her were unguarded in their comments.

'Isn't that a funny little horse?' she heard someone say as Priceless appeared on the screen.

'It doesn't gallop too well,' said another unidentified voice.

'Well it looks all right to me, it seems to be going quite well.' She recognised the American rider, Peter Green, as he made this last comment – but she kept a discreet silence, with an amused smile.

I had a fence in hand as we prepared for the show jumping. P was not displaying a great deal of enthusiasm when I began warming him up for the final phase in the stable area, but once we arrived in the collecting ring he sensed the big occasion and began jumping really well. It might be all right, I thought.

Once he arrived in the arena and realised that he had the chance to show off in front of a big audience, Priceless was really trying. I could feel his effort to get it right as he ballooned over the jumps to complete a clear round and give me a thrilling victory over Richard Meade on Kilcashel. At last, I felt, as I was presented with the Remy Martin Trophy, I had managed to get it together and produce the goods after eleven years.

I had a wonderful dinner with Uncle Jack, my mother, Dot and a few others that evening, which carried on long after they had been wise enough to go back to their beds. Louise Bates, Rachel Bayliss and I stayed on at the George Hotel in Stamford, keen to continue the celebrations.

'What would you like to drink?' asked Mary Charles, the manageress, whose kind hospitality we have greatly appreciated during the last few years. We all decided that we would love an Armagnac. Having finished that, another one seemed a splendid idea. And so it continued until Mary decided some blotting paper might be needed and presented us with a plate of delicious chicken sandwiches. Having kipped in the lorry for what was left of the night, I was feeling a little delicate the following day!

There was no celebration after I took Night Cap to my next contest at Weston Park. Maita Robinson, who helps us with all our paper-work and accounts at home, has not forgotten seeing me clear out the car with some gusto when I returned from the Staffordshire event.

'How did you do at the weekend?' she asked in all innocence.

I flung a couple of items over my shoulder and muttered, 'I jumped the wrong last fence if you *really* want to know.' As more objects went flying, she wisely retreated!

I was in a rage with myself. I had jumped the intermediate fence instead of the advanced, right at the end of the cross-country when Night Cap was about to win. Thankfully that stupid elimination was partially redeemed with a win at Chatsworth. One minute you're up, the next minute you're down – what a sport.

I was anxious to have a break when the season finished that year, to have a holiday in some place where the sun was shining, when Christopher Brooke turned up out of the blue. He had been a great friend back in the junior days and he suggested that I should go with him to Dubai, where he was working, and we could then go on for a holiday in Sri Lanka. It seemed – as it proved to be – a wonderful way to escape for a few weeks from the beginning of winter.

TEN

Preparing for the Olympics

For the second year running, Night Cap went to Badminton without Priceless. The selectors had asked me not ride P there as they were considering him for a place in the Olympics, which was my obvious goal for 1984. Similar requests were made to other riders whose horses had already proved themselves.

Using the new training schedule that I had prepared the previous summer, I was confident that N was as fit as he would ever be when we made our short journey of just over a mile down the road to Badminton and looked to see what snares Colonel Frank Weldon had in store for us on the cross-country course. I am never tempted to take a sneak preview; in fact, I'm so afraid that familiarity might breed contempt that I steer well clear of Badminton Park for at least a couple of months before the event takes place.

Night Cap's dressage was disappointing. He has a tendency to react to the big occasion – and particularly to the noise of people clapping – by boiling over and his test was below his best. He is capable of doing excellent dressage, so this problem with his highly-strung temperament was a real frustration. But his marks would not have made much difference that year, since I had a fall on the cross-country.

I had been in the television commentary box before I rode the cross-country, pleased to be asked back there after my initial effort at commentating during Burghley the previous year. While watching the monitor, I made up my mind as to how I would ride through the lake. I'd seen Lucinda and others land in the water and then take three strides to jump on to the platform and over the drop fence on top of it. That's the way to do it, I decided; I would land in the water and kick on to reach the platform in three strides.

The plan failed. N hit the rails on top of the bank, nose-dived towards the ground and was brilliant not to fall – nor to tread on me as I tumbled off. I remounted and he jumped the rest of the course quite beautifully, but it brought a return of the all too familiar self-doubt. I asked Lucinda, who won her sixth Badminton that year, what I had done wrong at the lake.

'You should never ever try to look for a stride through water,' she said.

It was a lesson worth learning, even though it had been taught to me the hard way. I should have sat still and made whatever adjustments were needed as we emerged from the water, as was quite plain when I later studied it on video.

After Badminton I found a prayer on the kitchen notice board in the bungalow, which had become my part of our home at Ivyleaze, and subsequently discovered that it had been pinned there by Dot. It read, 'Oh Lord, grant me the serenity to accept those things I cannot change, the courage to change the things I can and the wisdom to know the difference.' It couldn't have been more relevant.

I took Murphy Himself, then supposedly a six-year-old, to his first three-day event at Avenches in Switzerland the following month. Mark Phillips and Lorna Clarke were also competing, with Malcolm Wallace as our chef d'équipe. Louise Bates came with us for the fun of it, and I can't think of any trip that turned out to be quite such enormous fun.

One evening we went out to an old castle near Berne, owned by Hans Leonz-Notter and – after a lively dinner – we began playing with loaded pistols and rifles down in his cellar. Eventually we took it in turns to aim at an empty wine bottle. Mark and Malcolm (both of whom had been in the army and should therefore have had the advantage over the rest of us when it came to pointing a pistol) missed the target. Louise, Lorna and I hit it at the first attempt; we felt (and no doubt sounded) very smug about our combined achievement. Wol and Mark, of course, have never lived it down.

During another fantastic evening, Mark produced his special party trick. With a tumbler half-full of water balanced on his forehead, he invited us to bet on whether he could drink the water without touching the glass with his hands. Thinking this impossible, Roland Straub placed a bottle of champagne on the table and challenged Mark to try it with bubbly instead of water. With the bottle now balanced on his forehead, Mark lowered himself cautiously until he was first sitting and then lying on the floor. Grabbing the bottle between his knees with considerable athletic dexterity, he then lay it on its side by his shoulder and began drinking from it. Poor Roland was dumbfounded! Louise later procured the empty bottle and used it to make a lamp that will always remind her of Switzerland.

Throughout the trip, Mark Phillips called Louise and I by nicknames – I was either 'Bloodshot' or 'Chunky' and she was always referred to as 'Thunder-thighs'. Mummy and Dot didn't escape – Hinge and Bracket seemed the perfect choice. Eventually we all put our heads together and decided to retaliate; from thereon Mark was known as Phillis. We even blacked out the 'P' in his name on the side of his lorry and he drove around for days without realising what we had done. One of the gossip columnists wrote a piece about it, asking whether anyone could shed light on the reason why Mark's name had been changed, but Louise and I maintaned a guilty silence.

Our wonderful trip ended in the best possible way for me, because Murphy won. It wasn't a particularly important event and few people would have regarded my victory as a great achievement but, after all the soul-searching that followed Badminton, it seemed like a heaven-sent blessing.

Another blessing was the arrival from Australia of Claire Tweedie, whom we had first met through the friends we had made in the Philippines, David and Jenny Malcolm. Claire had come to stay with us for Badminton with the intention of making Ivyleaze her first stop on a grand tour of the world. We rather disrupted that plan by asking whether she would groom for us in Los Angeles if I were chosen for the Olympics. She is a trained nurse, a very good horsewoman, tremendously competent and a great friend. I would trust her as much as I would my mother or Dorothy. To my great delight, she said she would be thrilled to have an active part to play in the Olympics.

Although I didn't know it at the time, all but one of the companies in the British National Insurance Group had decided that it would be inappropriate for them to subscribe to the renewal of my contract when it expired in November later that year. The only reason why I wasn't brought in on these discussions was because I had such understanding sponsors; they were anxious to avoid giving me any cause for worry while I was aiming for the Olympics.

There was a very happy outcome for me since one of the companies in the group, British National Life Assurance, decided that it would be worthwhile for them to take over the sponsorship. Roger Davies, the managing director, showed his thoughtfulness very swiftly by giving me a three-year contract to sign in May, which was dated to commence six months later in November. In that way my future for the next three years was settled before I even had a chance to start worrying about it.

Meanwhile Night Cap's tendency to become over-wrought in the dressage on important occasions had been giving us food for thought. We decided to write to the organisers of the Bath and West Show at Shepton Mallet to ask whether we could take N there for the four days, so that he could learn how to cope with crowds and noise. The request was granted on condition that I agreed to lead the parade before the Shetland Pony Grand National, which suited me fine.

So we boxed him up on each of the four mornings and drove to Shepton Mallet, where we kept him on the showground from about nine o'clock in the morning until six in the evening. I rode him around at a walk, letting him listen to the band, watch the people jumping out of aeroplanes and have a look at the heavy horses and their vehicles in the hope that the Whitbread drays at Badminton would no longer hold any fears for him. He was in a muck sweat and totally impossible for the first three days of the Bath and West and I was utterly exhausted; on the fourth day he decided that the whole thing was a complete bore and he didn't bat an eyelid.

We decided that noise affected him far more than strange sights, so we looked to other ways of trying to overcome the frustrating problem. He is capable of doing excellent dressage and he finds it easy; perhaps if it were a little more difficult for him, his concentration wouldn't waver quite so easily. Anyway, we took him to some local football matches at Badminton; we went into the Park and played him a tape recording of a brass band; we persuaded about twenty people to come to Ivyleaze and clap continuously while I did some dressage on him; we played the brass band tape to him in his stable. Slowly but surely, at the end of about six months, he began to accept the noise without losing his cool.

While we were preparing for the final Olympic Trial at Castle Ashby in Northamptonshire, I went up to London to attend a dinner party which Malcolm Wallace was giving at the King's Troop Barracks in St John's Wood, where he was then commanding officer. His wife, Caroline, was away in Devon with the children and Wol had asked me to stand in for her. Half-way through dinner my lip suddenly blew up; then a lump appeared on my arm.

'I think I might have a problem, Wol,' I said.

He looked at me and asked, 'My God, what's happened to you?'

I had no idea what had happened, so I finished dinner and went off to the party that followed. About ten minutes later, I realised that I could scarcely speak, my lips were so swollen, and I looked dreadful.

'I think I'd better leave,' I said to Wol.

He took another horrified look at me and put me into a taxi which took me to Mary Gordon-Watson's flat in London, where I was due to spend the night. I am told that after I left someone asked, 'Who was that woman?'

Always ready for a bit of devilment, Wol said, 'I've no idea, never seen her before in my life!'

I fell asleep in Mary's flat and woke in the middle of the night to find myself covered in huge lumps and itching from head to toe. In the morning Mary covered me in calamine lotion, which gave me some relief, before I went to Harley Street and then to the hospital for skin diseases in London. They reckoned that the lumps were caused by the sun, which seemed highly unlikely to me since I had spent a good deal of my life in hot climates without suffering any ill effects.

The irritation brought me close to screaming point as I drove myself back to Acton Turville that day. At home I couldn't sleep and could hardly bear to move; any time material touched my skin, I felt like screaming. Louise came down to stay; she and my mother spent many hours (sometimes by the light of a torch) gathering dock leaves in the garden. They were fed into the Magimix with a splash of vinegar to produce a sticky mess that was then spread all over me until I looked like the Green Giant. I took a bath about once an hour to try to cool my inflamed skin, which kept blowing up into massive lumps until I thought they would burst.

Meanwhile, I had been to see a specialist in Bristol, Dr Warin, who was taking various tests and prescribing different pills in the hope of finding something that would work. Adrenalin injections gave me temporary relief from the unbearable itching, but they made my heart beat at a furious pace and brought on an uncontrollable twitching as though I'd had too many brandies. Unless some effective treatment could be found fairly quickly, I was in danger of missing the Olympics. My mother was at her wit's end wondering what could be done for me.

Eventually we discovered, thanks to the specialist, some very strong anti-histamine tablets that reduced the swellings. They also made me feel unbelievably tired, which would have been fine if I hadn't been aiming for the Olympics. I felt as weak as a kitten when I rode – for the first time since the problem started – just three days before the final Olympic Trial was to take place at Castle Ashby. Everyone said I looked worn out and ill when I arrived at the Northamptonshire venue, which was a fairly accurate description of how I felt.

By some miracle, the horses went well; Night Cap won and Priceless jumped a deliberately steady clear round. I very nearly passed out when I finished the cross-country course with N (who was the second of my two rides) and there was no temptation to stay up half the night celebrating on Armagnac! I felt tired enough to sleep for a week. Both the horses were chosen to make the trip to Los Angeles and I had to continue taking the same number of anti-histamine tablets; if I tried to reduce the dosage, the lumps began to reappear. It didn't seem the best way to set out for the Olympics, but obviously I had told those who needed to know and, fortunately, the soporific effects began to wear off so that I was feeling a bit more alert when we assembled at Wylye for the final training under the eagle eye of the selectors, chef d'équipe Wol, plus Peter and Ann Scott-Dunn, who do such a wonderful job keeping a strict eye on the horses' fitness and well-being.

I had been chosen with Lucinda Green, Ian Stark, Tiny Clapham and Robert Lemieux. The team of four was to be chosen after we arrived in Los Angeles but, even though we knew that one of us would be dropped, there was a wonderful sense of camaraderie rather than competition as we prepared our horses for the great event. It was again tempting to do too much, to feel that you should be working like crazy during the last few weeks that were left. Remembering how Night Cap had sunk in the river bed when I had been plagued by similar feelings a year earlier, I managed to restrain myself.

To my great delight I had been told that Dorothy was to be one of our two official team trainers in Los Angeles, together with Ferdi Eilberg. Sadly, Lady Hugh Russell and her famous mini-moke would not be coming with us, but she was at home in Wylye to help us with the final cross-country schooling in between arranging for us to be served with scrumptious food. Pat Burgess came to Wylye each day and helped us to get our horses jumping more athletically. As usual, she also helped to prepare my mind for a positive approach to the challenge that lay ahead.

In case all this suggests an over-earnest dedication, I should add that we had great fun. Malcolm Wallace manages to combine his meticulous attention to detail with a relaxed and wonderful sense of humour, while the rest of my companions were not noticeably reluctant to have a laugh. It was a time of exhilaration as well as serious training.

My own nervous misgivings did nothing to lessen the excitement of going with Tiny Clapham to London to collect our Olympic uniforms – blue trousers, white Aertex shirt and white sweater with the

Olympic rings – nor of putting it on for the departure to Los Angeles. By then my mother and Dot had already left to pick up the camper that was to be their mobile home during the Games. Claire had also gone ahead with the two horses.

Christopher Brooke, who again turned up out of the blue from Dubai, drove me to the airport, where I felt as conspicuous as someone in fancy dress. Without my realising it Chris had slipped a bottle of champagne into my overnight bag, but his wonderful gesture was somewhat marred when the bag was put down a little too firmly and the bottle broke. My nightie, washbag and books I had taken to read were soaked in champagne.

By then I had met my pals and was doing my best to mop up when the others went on their separate ways to do some duty-free shopping. When some of the group met up with me again, they found me searching frantically – and in vain – for my boarding pass. Our team vet, Peter Scott-Dunn, and his wife, Ann, the dressage rider and trainer, Ferdi Eilberg, helped in the search – but to no avail.

'You will just have to talk your way through,' they told me.

That was easier said than done. I was told that on no account would I be allowed on the plane unless I could produce my boarding pass. I had horrible visions of seeing the Olympic three-day event team leave without me; the necessary piece of paper was still nowhere to be found. Eventually, while the Scott-Dunns held the steward in conversation, I managed to sneak past. The relief was immense. This was a fine way to start my Olympic campaign.

I never did find the boarding pass, but I found plenty of unbroken bottles of champagne. Each of the other riders, making their independent way through the duty-free shop, had decided to buy me a replacement. If anyone were looking for an example of wonderful team spirit, that was it. We had a very giggly trip. Lucinda and I, when asked by a fellow Olympian what sport we represented, replied, 'Shot putt, of course,' showing our muscles. To our horror he said, 'How silly of me, I should have known by looking at you.'

When we arrived in Los Angeles, we were all taken to a huge balloon-shaped marquee where we were given our accreditations. As the identifying piece of plastic was hung around my neck, the extraordinary dream became a reality – I had arrived and I was actually labelled as one of the Olympians.

From Los Angeles, we took a bus to the stables at Santa Anita. Poor Claire Tweedie and the other girls who were grooming looked hot and tired; each of their tiny shared rooms above the stables was equipped with just one small fan and they can't have had a comfortable stay, but they were all making sure that the horses had every possible attention. I knew that Priceless and Night Cap were in Claire's capable hands and that she would also be the close friend to whom I could talk in times of stress.

The riders lived in luxury. Malcolm Wallace had arranged for us to stay in a rented house in Santa Anita through Tony and Tricia Rice (she was formerly Mrs Brands and the mother of Dawn, with whom I had competed in my junior days) and we had every comfort, including a swimming pool, where we spent most of our afternoons before the event began. The grooms welcomed the opportunity to come and join us there to cool off. My mother, staying with Dot in the camper that was parked outside the house, became our cook and washer-woman. The food she produced was marvellous, but our clothes tended to change colour when passing through her hands!

We were only about fifteen minutes' drive from the stables and, since we would be working the horses early each morning before the heat of the day, it obviously suited us better than staying more than an hour's drive away in the Olympic Village, much as we would have liked to savour the atmosphere. Even so, we had to be up soon after 5 a.m. each morning in order to start riding the horses at six o'clock – and, partly because of the pills I was still having to take, I found that very tiring.

Our two team trainers were there to help us during those early morning sessions. Dorothy looked after me and Ian Stark while we worked our horses on the flat, always conscious of the big responsibility that was creeping ever nearer. Priceless did not exactly help to boost my confidence when, during the final week, he decided that he could no longer do counter canter; every time I attempted that loop of the serpentine where he should have been leading on his outside leg, he did a flying change.

'This is *hopeless*,' I said to Dorothy, who was always a calming presence, whether out in one of the practice arenas or back at the stables, where her knowledge and her eagle eye proved invaluable. Eventually I decided that I must take a grip on myself and not become obsessed by the counter canter problem; I would just have to hope and pray that it would come right – and, thankfully, it did.

Santa Anita racecourse, which was the venue for all the equestrian events apart from our cross-country, is a lovely natural amphitheatre, surrounded by mountains. There was every facility we could possibly require – for schooling, jumping, galloping or for a relaxed hack around the outside of the racecourse. By the time the horses had been returned to their stables after their early morning exercise, we were more than ready to do justice to the incredible breakfast which the organisers had prepared for us.

The choice was unbelievable: fresh melons, strawberries, a selection of cereals, Danish pastries, scrambled egg, potato cakes, bacon sausages, tomatoes, toast and croissants – everything that you could possibly wish for was ready and waiting for us to help ourselves. We would leave the breakfast table feeling several pounds heavier and I'm sure Ian Stark was the only Olympian in history to gain a stone in weight during the Games. Apart from the daily skipping or running which most of us did, we were able to relax until the next early morning call from our alarm clocks.

The one really distressing part of the tight security in operation for the Olympic Games was that my mother couldn't see her own horses at all during the first week. That hurt me dreadfully; she had been the one to make all the sacrifices to get me to the Games and now some stupid rule was barring the owners from the stables and practice areas. I felt cut in half, I was so desperately upset for her. Eventually it was agreed that the owners would be allowed in at certain times of the day, but it still galls me that something so important should have been totally mismanaged. It was only through relentless badgering by our Director-General, Jack Reynolds, and Wol that they eventually succumbed.

We had to travel 100 miles to Fairbanks Ranch near San Diego for the riders' briefing (and for our first view of the cross-country fences that had been built there) because the climate was cooler than in Santa Anita, where the dressage and show jumping were to take place. There didn't seem to be much of a drop in temperature as we sat through the briefing, which took twice as long as usual, before taking a dusty ride in cattle trucks around the roads and tracks. We looked like a bunch of grubby urchins by the time we walked the steeplechase and cross-country courses. The beautifully built fences (designed by Neil Ayer) were alarming on the first inspection. Having met my mother and the Rices that evening, we developed a lasting taste for margaritas, and, when we viewed the fences the following morning they looked infinitely better.

Meanwhile our team had been chosen. Robert Lemieux was omitted and whatever disappointment he might have felt was submerged; he promptly became a marvellous support to the rest of us. I was chosen with Priceless, since he was the more experienced of the two horses.

Deciding on the order in which we would ride was the next conundrum and, as usual, Malcolm Wallace consulted us about the decision that had to be made.

It seemed right that Ian Stark should go second, as is customary for anyone new to the team, but that still left various permutations which we discussed among ourselves. If Tiny Clapham went first on Windjammer – and she was perfectly prepared to do so – Lucinda Green could go in her favourite third spot on Regal Realm and I could go last on Priceless. But going first had not worked well the previous year for Tiny when she had her fall in Frauenfeld; it seemed better for her to go third. On that basis, Lucinda and I would go first and last – but in which order? Lucinda was our top rider and bang on form; it seemed a waste to put her first (though she, too, was perfectly willing) when we knew that she would have a better chance of an individual medal if she went later.

So I said that I would go first, leaving Ian, Tiny and Lucinda to follow in that order. Malcolm was happy with this arrangement, so the order was settled. It had not been an easy decision. I had asked the Good Lord for guidance without seeming to receive any clear message – except for both my mother and Dorothy pointing out that things had worked well on the two previous occasions when I went first for the team. I have to confess to a moment of anguish after the die was cast.

We felt tremendously proud of Lucinda when we heard that she had been chosen, through the unanimous decision of the British Olympic Committee, to carry our flag at the opening ceremony. I was longing to go with her to the Olympic Stadium for this great occasion, but there was strong argument against it: the buses would not be back in Santa Anita until midnight and I had an early date in the dressage arena the following morning. I would have to be up at 5 a.m. in order to start working Priceless at six o'clock.

'I honestly think you'd be a twit to come,' said Lucinda, while I was still dithering.

I was torn between wanting to support her and the knowledge that it would be wise to have an early night. I had actually changed in readiness to go with her when Robert Lemieux decided he would attend the opening ceremony. Ian and Tiny, already feeling the effects of the heat in Santa Anita and reckoning that the temperature in the Olympic Stadium would be more than they could stand, stayed behind with me.

As I watched the ceremony on television, I realised that the moment of truth had almost arrived.

108

ELEVEN
The Olympic Three-Day Event

'Please can you get me some water, because I'm feeling incredibly faint,' I said to Malcolm Wallace, shortly before I was due into the dressage arena for the first phase of the Olympic Three-Day Event. Actually I felt a margarita would have been more suitable.

I had been working Priceless for about an hour, wearing my tail coat, and the heat proved too much for me even though it was still early morning. I suddenly felt as though I might pass out. Fortunately there were water points spread out around the Santa Anita racetrack and Wol was able to comply with my request swiftly. I drank some water and, thank God, felt normal again. Wol, greatly relieved, then jokingly said, 'What a wimp!'

Priceless was the third horse into the arena and he did a good dressage test, apart from making a bosh of the right half-pass in which he put in one unscheduled stride at canter. Although I felt I could have done a little better, I was reasonably pleased with our performance which, with the mark of 56.4 penalties, was to leave us equal seventh of the forty-eight competitors when the two days of dressage were completed.

My brother, Michael, and his wife, Fiona, were among the spectators. It had been a great and unexpected thrill when they arrived to add to the family support from my mother and Uncle Jack. To everyone's amazement, Michael took a keen and intelligent interest throughout the two days of dressage, which usually bores anyone who is not closely involved with horses. He loved the cross-country, but it was the dressage that really fascinated him.

Dorothy was delighted. 'He's the only member of the family who could make a top dressage rider, because he has the patience,' she said to my mother. Was she trying to tell me something?

We all watched Ian Stark, who finished on exactly the same score as me to become joint seventh, and we suffered agonies with Tiny Clapham the following day when Windjammer began to boil over while the audience gave her some far from helpful applause during the test. She finished the dressage on 70 penalties. Lucinda had insisted that we shouldn't wait for her test on Regal Realm, that we could use the time more profitably by heading south for the Fairbanks Ranch (the former home of Douglas Fairbanks) and having another walk around the cross-country course that same afternoon. As we learnt later, it was generally reckoned that Lucinda was harshly marked for 63.8 penalties. Switzerland's Hansueli Schmutz held the individual lead with 39.8 on his 1981 European Champion Oran at the end of the dressage; the USA headed the eleven teams and we were in fourth place.

Because of the distance between the two venues there was an unaccustomed rest day separating the dressage and cross-country, which gave me the opportunity for a fourth and last look at the fences designed by Neil Ayer. On the night before the cross-country, I sat in bed with the map of the course and a tape recorder in front of me, speaking my thoughts aloud as I went round the entire course in my head. I recorded every single detail that I could remember about each fence – the approach, the exact number of trees, where I should turn, etc – then I listened to the tape as I played and replayed it.

Finally I rang up Louise, who was awakened in the middle of the night back home in England to hear my nervous voice saying, 'Batesy, I'm feeling awfully scared!'

'Hello Gin,' she said, as she emerged from her sleep. 'Is everything all right?'

'Yes, everything's fine,' I replied in the same nervous tone.

She was a marvellous pal, full of chat and eager to know all the ins-and-outs of what had happened so far. 'I'm sure you'll be fine,' she said, and made me promise to phone her again the following night.

I had to leave the hotel very early the next morning with Malcolm Wallace and Peter Scott-Dunn, and I had a nasty fright when we were delayed by a traffic jam no one had anticipated. To the horror of Peter and myself, Wol then decided to show his hand at rally driving. As a result we reached the stables in plenty of time, to find Claire, Dot and Priceless ready and waiting.

Anyone who was up early enough to watch P on the roads and tracks could have been forgiven for wondering whether he was fit enough to cover the entire journey of 16½ miles (26,465 metres), let alone jump the steeplechase and cross-country fences. He worried me, even though I should know better, as he set out in a rather sullen trot. I had no need to restrain him on the first 2½-mile section of roads and tracks; he had decided the pace we should go and I let him get on with it, while the usual fears flashed through my mind: have I made a monumental mistake and failed to get him fit enough?

He became very excited, as he always does, when he saw the steeplechase course and he galloped over its 2 miles within the optimum time. Then he promptly reverted to his sullen trot for the second – and longer – 7½-mile section of roads and tracks. At a given point there was supposed to be someone to put water on the horses, and I felt that Priceless needed it. I arrived at the appointed spot to find an Italian and Frenchman waiting, who didn't have a clue what I was talking about when I asked them to slosh some cooling water on my horse. Eventually, one of them put his hand in the bucket and stroked P's neck with his wet hand, which was not quite what I had in mind.

As I should have known, Priceless had the whole thing sussed out. He is unbelievably intelligent; he knows exactly the speed required for each part of the journey and uses his uninspiring-looking trot around the roads and tracks as a means of conserving energy. Back in the Box for the ten-minute halt, he wore a lethargic look while everyone did what was necessary – checking his shoes, hosing him down, applying grease to his forelegs so that they would slide over any fence he might hit and so on. He finally changed from zombie to lion as I got back on him. Rearing and behaving like a fool, he nearly bowled over our precious chef d'équipe.

He was superb across country and, though I wasn't aiming to go particularly fast, he completed the 4½ miles within a second of the optimum time for just 0.4 of a penalty. I felt giddy with elation as I finished and dismounted, before rushing up to Malcolm Wallace and saying, breathlessly, 'Wol, I've got so much to tell you.'

'Calm down, Ginny,' he said, 'there's plenty of time. Just sit down quietly and have a drink, then we'll talk about it.'

I'd completely forgotten there was at least an hour before Ian came into the Box. Having had my quiet drink, I told Wol that I'd had a problem at the Bridge and Walkway, fence seven, which was basically a stretch of water with a Normandy bank in the middle. In this case you had to look for a stride after landing in the water, because the Normandy bank was only a stride or two away; there was no room to leave the horse to its own devices as I should have done when riding Night Cap through the lake at Badminton. Having deliberated over this fence for a long time when we walked the course, we had decided it would be better to take two strides in the water. It would give the horse time to get used to the splashing and to see the jump ahead – so

111

that became our plan A.

Priceless decided differently. He took one stride only, jumped on to the Normandy bank from a long way back and left one hind leg behind as he landed. Thanks to his athleticism, which enables him to get out of trouble, and verbal encouragement from the rider, he went safely over the rails on top of the bank to jump back into the water, but it was an undeniably awkward moment. I said that plan B would have to be put into action, that the others should go for only one stride. Princess Anne, who was stationed at the same fence and sending back valuable information, said the same.

I also told Wol that I had been a bit slow when I looked at my stop-watch half-way round the course, but had managed to make up the time to finish with just that 0.4 of a penalty. I therefore suggested that the others didn't go flat out on the first half, that they waited to see how much petrol they had left, because there were galloping stretches from there to the finish and it was possible to make up for any lost time. My only other relevant item of information was the fact that the dry grass was surprisingly slippery on the turns and that it was like riding in a sauna.

Wol briefed the three other riders when they came into the Box for the ten-minute halt, while I hovered nearby (by now sporting my cool Union Jack shorts) in case anyone wanted to talk to me. I had a brief, slightly nervous chatter with each of them and then ran over part of the course, so that I could see them over as many fences as possible. While I was running to watch Ian Stark, I heard someone shout my name. It was my brother, Michael. I hadn't seen him since my own cross-country round and felt really touched by his emotion when he said, 'I feel so proud of you.'

Ian followed Wol's instructions and rode a steady clear round on Oxford Blue. Then Tiny Clapham, the next to go for our team, had a fall in the water at fence seven, before remounting Windjammer in her wet and slippery clothes, to complete the course. No one could have taken that disappointment better than she did. She had dismissed her own ambitions by the time I helped to yank off her wet clothes and find a pair of Union Jack shorts for her; she wanted to get straight back out on the course and support the team.

I had so much faith in Lucinda's ability that I was convinced she would jump a fast clear round on Regal Realm before she had even left the Box. It was a source of pride, but not in the least surprising, when she recorded one of the only three rounds with neither jumping nor time penalties. Sadly, because of the harsh dressage marks, she had

9a. Night Cap on the cross-country course at Burghley, 1984, which we won (*Kit Houghton*)

9b. Holiday time for the two boys – Priceless (*left*) and Night Cap (*Barn Owl*)

10a. Priceless in the dressage arena at Badminton, 1985 (*Kit Houghton*)

10b. Badminton, 1985.
Night Cap attacks the Fairbanks
Bounce, the first of two fences
that had really worried me
(*Kit Houghton*)

10c. Two good boys!
Priceless and Night Cap
finish first and third
at Badminton
(*Barn Owl*)

11a. Priceless trying his hardest in the Badminton show jumping, 1985 (*Colorsport*)

11b. Priceless looking pleased with himself as he inspects the Whitbread Trophy, Badminton, 1985 (*Colorsport*)

12a. Riding Murphy Himself at Iping, 1985,
with a splint to protect the left wrist
I had cracked three days earlier
(*Kit Houghton*)

12b. Priceless sails over Centaur's Leap
on his way to winning the 1985
European Championships at Burghley
(*Barn Owl*)

13. Mission accomplished!
(*Gypsy Joe*)

14a. Doing my best to look like Jerry Hall at the Woburn Abbey fashion show (*Kit Houghton*)

14b. 'Here come some more black clouds,' I told Devina Cannon, who was suitably dressed for the 1986 Badminton (*Kit Houghton*)

15a. Priceless's tail swishing furiously after making a mistake at the first cross-country fence in the World Championships at Gawler, Australia, 1986

15b. Priceless over Fence 4, the Loading Platform. He settled down to jump a fantastic round (*Jim Meads*)

16a. Great Britain's gold-medal team
at the World Championships
(*left to right*): Lorna Clarke and Myross,
myself and Priceless, Ian Stark and Oxford Blue,
Clissy Strachan and Delphy Dazzle
(*Jim Meads*)

16b. Priceless's breeder, Diana Scott,
pours the victory champagne
for my mother, myself and Dot

no chance of moving into the lead as the result of this marvellous performance and was lying eighth when the cross-country was completed. The overnight leader, Hansueli Schmutz, had lost his chance of an individual medal when Oran stopped on the Normandy bank at the influential seventh fence, leaving Karen Stives (USA) in front on Ben Arthur. Mark Todd was lying second for New Zealand on Charisma and I was third on Priceless. The more important team scores showed that Britain was now a close second, less than two show jumping fences behind the USA.

I made my promised call to Louise Bates that evening, which was again in the not-too-early hours of the morning for her in England. She had watched the television and knew the bare bones of what had happened, but was eager to be filled in with all the details. I wasn't necessarily making more sense, but I was certainly sounding less nervous than I had been twenty-four hours earlier.

Prince Philip was there to chat to us during the veterinary inspection which took place the following morning, before the horses were loaded into a convoy of lorries to be driven back to Santa Anita. Having seen them off, the British riders and their chef d'équipe filled in the second unaccustomed rest day (this time between the cross-country and show jumping) by making pigs of ourselves. First we ate a massive quantity of ice-cream and then, on the journey back to Santa Anita, the riders decided that Wol must be introduced to American fast food. So we stopped for McDonald's hamburgers and chocolate milk shakes. The subsequent nausea suggested that the day's diet could have been better chosen!

On our return, we checked the horses and took them out for a short walk. Jennie Loriston-Clark, who was competing in our dressage team, had kindly exercised Night Cap for me during my absence, with me hoping that he would turn into a Grand Prix dressage horse overnight. Both he and Priceless were looking fit and well. Then we had our first look at the show jumping course, which seemed amazingly small, although we later discovered that it was at maximum height. The minuscule impression came from the fact that most of the fences were at least twice as wide (from left to right rather than from take-off to landing) than anything we had seen before. Mark Todd was a lone figure in the grandstand as we walked round the course. He was no doubt feeling as nervous as the rest of us. 'Looking at the fences won't do much good, Toddy,' I yelled to him, aware that my own heart was in my mouth.

I must have walked the show jumping course about fifteen times, and we all signed the blackboard under one of the fences, before I joined Michael in the grandstand to watch the early competitors jumping in the reverse order of merit. It felt like the longest day in my life. My brother and I were trying to occupy ourselves by working out how long it would take me to walk back to the stables, have a shower,

get changed into riding clothes (including the breeches and coat that Harry Hall had kindly given to all the team members), get on Priceless, work him in, complete the show jumping. It was a totally unnecessary exercise, since I'd already decided what time I should leave the grandstand, but it helped to fill in all those minutes that seemed like hours while I was waiting.

Peter Robeson (who was in Los Angeles to help the British show jumpers) and Ted Edgar (who was doing the same for the Australians) came into the practice area to give us the benefit of their expertise. The course must have looked ridiculously small compared with the sort they're used to inspecting, but they completely understood how important that final phase was to the British three-day event team and they were tremendously helpful.

I watched Tiny jump her clear round on Windjammer, but was already warming up for my own round when Lucinda went clear on Regal Realm (to finish sixth) and when Ian had his one mistake on Oxford Blue (who was ninth). Priceless knew the occasion warranted a special effort and he had no intention of touching anything, even in the practice area.

'That's great,' said Peter Robeson, after I had jumped only half a dozen practice fences. 'Leave him as he is, you don't need to do any more.'

Peter must have been right, because Priceless was still trying his hardest when he went into the arena and jumped a clear round. There were tears – of relief as much as happiness – from my mother, Dot, Claire and myself as I rode out knowing that I had won an individual medal. I was hugged by everybody and then walked with Wol, through the tunnel and into the grandstand, holding his hand like a small child.

I was in time to watch Mark Todd jump his last few fences on Charisma and to know, from the roar of the crowds, that he was clear. Lucinda and I were together as we watched American's Karen Stives come in for the final and decisive round of the competition on Ben Arthur. Karen was under tremendous pressure: if she hit one fence, she would lose the individual gold to Mark Todd; if she hit two, the United States would lose the team gold to Britain.

The middle of the treble, the second last fence, was the only one to

114

fall. Lucinda and I screamed with joy for Toddy; he is tremendously popular in England, where he spends so much of his time, and we felt we were cheering for one of our own. Despite the fierce heat of the Californian sun, the thrill of Mark's win brought me out in goose pimples. Someone actually asked me, in tones of amazement, whether I was feeling cold.

I asked Karen Stives, who has since become a great friend of mine, how she felt when she was under so much pressure. Apparently, she was worried that she might get herself into a dreadful state of nerves, so had decided to forget about it and pretend she was jumping at home. Since Ben Arthur was not a particularly reliable showjumper, she didn't expect to win, and was delighted with an individual silver to go with her team gold medal.

Toddy had won with 51.6 penalties, Karen was second (54.2) and I was third (56.8). The stirring Olympic theme music was playing as the three of us rode in to receive our individual medals, making it an unforgettably emotional moment. It was equally emotive to hear our own national anthems played as we stood on the podium, before the chosen dignitary made the presentations. After he had put the ribbon around my neck, I shook his hand and kissed him on both cheeks.

Prince Philip then came forward to present us all with bouquets of flowers. This *has* to be my big chance, I thought, as I waited for him to reach the bronze medallist. He must have known what was in my mind; having presented the flowers and shaken my hand, Prince Philip took a nimble step backwards. Never mind, I told myself, there's still one more chance!

The United States had won, beating us by just 3.2 penalties, with Germany a distant third. I was with my team mates when I returned to the Olympic podium and this time Jean Duc de Luxembourg made the presentations. He, too, received a kiss on both cheeks – while Prince Philip watched me with a wary eye as he waited to hand out more bouquets of flowers. When he reached the silver medal team, he looked at me and said, 'I'll kiss you some other time.' I promptly giggled like a schoolgirl.

It was just as well that he didn't visit the stable area after the presentations. He would have found the riders either racing around in the golf buggies that had been provided for our local transport or participating in the most almighty water fight – which became totally out of hand after someone had the bright idea of using the fire hose. Mark Todd was debagged and left in only his underpants; the rest of us, though fully dressed, were soaked to the skin.

We were looking rather more respectable when we went to the roof garden of a hotel to be interviewed by Russell Harty for one of the programmes he was presenting from Los Angeles. The invitation had come about through my sister-in-law, Fiona, who had worked with him as his producer. 'Why don't you interview the British three-day event team?' she had asked Russell Harty, when meeting him in LA.

He had followed up the suggestion and was talking to us beside the roof garden swimming pool. The heat was almost unbearable and we longed to plunge into the water; I could feel trickles of sweat running down my back as I stood, with an orange juice in my hand, trying to look suitably cool for the interview.

A few days after our competition was over we were invited, through Samantha Eggar (who is an actress and step-sister of Vivien, my great friend in Singapore), to watch a polo match at the Griffiths Park Equestrian Centre. It was called Polo for Pandas and had been arranged to support the World Wildlife Fund. Prince Philip also happened to be there and, when he saw me, he came across and said, 'I suppose you've come for a congratulatory award?'

'Yes please,' I answered, so he gave me a peck on the cheek.

'Don't go away,' I begged him, 'because I know Lucinda and Tiny would like one as well.'

They were both nearby and they came rushing forward together in response to my signal.

'I suppose,' said Prince Philip, laughing, 'that the silver medallists deserve something.' So they both had a peck on the cheek as well. In typical royal family style, Prince Philip made three people incredibly happy. What would our country do without them?

Mohammed Ali was also at the Polo for Pandas match and, by now full of boldness, I walked across and chatted to him. His face was smooth as a baby's without the hint of a line on it – and, though I don't think his wife was too pleased with me, he was marvellous.

On another occasion, we went to a party in Hollywood, given by Anthony and Georgina Andrews, and I found myself chatting to the Colonel from MASH and to Joan Collins's sister Jackie, who was very interesting in a remarkably forthright way. The main reason for the party was to promote Caroline Wallace's bronzes, which were on display and much admired; I have since become the proud owner of a lovely one of Priceless.

We had stayed on in the rented house at Santa Anita after our competition was over. It had been offered to the show jumpers, whose contests came later in the Games, so that they could be near the

116

stables, but they elected to remain in the Olympic Village. We still saw a fair amount of them and were grateful for the way they rooted for us, even travelling to Fairbanks Ranch to lend their support on cross-country day.

Steven Smith became the badge broker of the British Equestrian Team. National badges, especially those of the more remote countries, were selling for up to $500 on the streets of Los Angeles and it didn't take Harvey's show jumping son long to get the whole thing sussed out. 'I'll have five of those for one of these,' he would say, once his exchange was in full swing.

Our team took a trip to Disneyland with Steven and the two Whitaker brothers from the show jumping side. Wol instantly turned into a schoolboy and we stayed for about three times longer than intended. We had a go on everything, including the terrifying Space Mountain Ride on which I sat next to John Whitaker.

'Let me out,' he shouted, as he clutched my arm.

'You're supposed to be protecting me,' I told him, clutching the side rails until the whites of my knuckles showed.

When the hair-raising ride was over, Steven Smith walked nonchalantly out and said, 'What's everyone getting excited about? I thought it was boring.'

We weren't going to let him get away with that sort of crack too easily, so we retaliated by dragging him off to see Snow White and the Seven Dwarfs!

Needless to say, we were glued to our seats in the grandstand while the show jumpers were competing. Before the team contest Harvey Smith (who was out there to support Steven and to make his contribution to the television commentary) said to me, 'Right lass, you'd better come in and look at these fences.'

I walked into the arena with him and looked in dumb amazement at the course our show jumping riders would have to face. David Broome has suggested that event riders must be barmy to jump the solid cross-country fences that are constructed for us – but I know which I prefer! We 'barmy' eventers (excluding Lucinda who had already flown home) sat with the show jumpers during their competitions and we cheered ourselves hoarse when they won the team silver.

We also watched the dressage – including the German Dr Reiner Klimke's magical performance to win on Ahlerich – and we were in the stands of the Olympic stadium to watch Zola Budd's famous confrontation with Mary Decker. After the American girl had tripped on Zola's heel and gone sprawling, we had to do our own sprint out of the stadium to catch a bus for the Olympic Village. Once there, we would change into smarter clothes and go to a party which Princess Anne was attending. 'You must *not* be late,' Wol had told us.

The timing was tight, but we had reckoned we could watch Zola Budd's race and, as long as we made a hasty exit, still be in time for the party. The bus was waiting so Tiny, Ian, Robert, Caroline (otherwise known as Mrs Wol) and I leapt on to it, thankful that our tight schedule seemed to be working out. But the bus didn't move. It was unpleasantly smelly inside and no one would open the windows, because the athletes on board were still warm and they didn't want to get their muscles cold. Having sat for what seemed like hours in the stifling atmosphere we asked why, for heaven's sake, we weren't moving?

'We have a problem,' said the security guard on the bus, refusing to divulge any further information.

Another ten minutes went by, then one of the massive shot putters stood up and began to make menacing noises because he, too, was keen to get going. To our relief, the bus started moving. To our horror, it stopped again in downtown Los Angeles and we weren't allowed to get out. By now we were in a panic about the time, so I opened a window and leapt out – and the rest of our group followed. There was instant commotion and the wailing of a police siren.

Apparently the security guard's 'problem' concerned an instruction that, for political reasons, the Turks and Armenians must not be allowed to travel on the same bus, and it was thought that people from both countries were on board. Our nationality had not been questioned until we leapt through the window; it was then assumed that we must be Turks dressed up as Brits, with forged (or stolen) accreditation cards. There had already been one serious bomb scare and we seemed, inadvertently, to be causing another.

When the policemen rushed from their car to question us, we explained that we had been held up for ages and were late for an important party.

'Are you the Turks?' they asked.

'No,' we said, brandishing our accreditations, 'we're British.'

Fortunately, they saw the funny side and offered us a lift. The five of us and two policemen then squeezed into one car (with me sitting on the knee of an LA cop) and other motorists on the road gave an incredulous double-take as they drove past. We were, of course, late for the party.

Having apologised for our late arrival, we recounted what had happened.

'Now we've heard it all!' said Princess Anne and Wol. Like everyone else present, they didn't believe a word we were saying and thought that we'd invented the whole thing as an elaborate excuse!

After the closing ceremony had brought the twenty-third Olympiad to its colourful end, an exhausted group from the equestrian team flew back to Heathrow. We were interviewed, wearing our track suits and our medals, before I linked up with Louise Bates, who was there to drive me home.

'You'd better have a kip,' she said, as we headed west along the M4. I protested that I was far too excited, that I would much rather talk. But she didn't seem too keen on listening, or shouting, above the noise of the engine and I was certainly very tired. It wasn't long before I fell asleep in the passenger seat. I later discovered that this was all part of a preconceived plan worked out in collusion with my mother and Dot, who were already home. Louise was to park at the end of our drive, slip the Olympic medals and rosettes to someone while I was still asleep, and then wake me up at a given signal.

'We've arrived,' she said, giving me a shake.

I opened my eyes to the most incredible homecoming that anyone could possibly imagine. There was a ribbon at the bottom of the drive which I had to cut; there were television cameras, 'welcome home' banners that our local policeman had climbed up trees to hang in place, huge cardboard Olympic rings, balloons and streamers. Everyone from the village was there to greet me and to shower me with presents. I was given a lovely bronze figure of a girl on a pony, champagne, flowers, chocolates and carrots for Priceless, who had returned a couple of days earlier. He and Claire were among those waiting for my return − P in his Olympic rug, wearing the medals and rosettes which had been secreted from the car. It was a truly wonderful homecoming.

Needless to say, the champagne bottles were swiftly opened and we all had a drink. Indeed, the corks were popping for a long time, as the afternoon's celebrations merged into an evening party at which Lord and Lady Hugh Russell (having missed the Olympics and being eager for the blow-by-blow account I was all too ready to give) were among the guests we welcomed. At some stage in all these proceedings, I was dumped in the water trough.

119

TWELVE
Home and abroad

Priceless stayed in work for about ten days after his return from the Olympics. It has always been our policy to let the horses wind down from peak fitness with some daily exercise that slowly decreases before we turn them out to grass. P obviously thought his rest was overdue, because he became even more impossible than usual to catch. We always leave a headcollar on him, with a few inches of rope attached to it, and we follow a set ritual when we want to bring him in.

This means going into the field with the nut bowl and allowing him to take a mouthful from it without attempting to catch him; if you were to make the slightest move towards that short piece of rope at this stage, he would instantly whip round and be off, leaving you with a handful of air. Instead, you have to walk away, knowing that he will follow for a second mouthful of nuts. As before, you let him help himself and again walk away. It is only when he comes after you and takes his third mouthful that you can reach for the rope and, you hope, catch him. It's a pathetic routine but unfortunately necessary.

Night Cap, who is far too gentlemanly to give you this sort of hassle, remained in training after the Games. I was hoping that he would help me to follow the instructions contained in a telegram from Charles Stratton, director of the Burghley Three-Day Event, that had been sent to me in Los Angeles. It read, 'Congratulations and well done. Now come and win your second Burghley.'

Other valued messages of congratulations were less specific about my next goal. There was a smashing card from Sir Robin Day, whom I had sat beside at a dinner many years earlier; Olive Oyl (Christopher Brooke's fantastic pony) sent me a telegram; Susan Piggott wrote to send me her own and Lester's best wishes; Cherry Hatton-Hall, my former instructor at Benenden, sent me a lovely letter from the London Convent where she is now a nun. There were even two letters from East Germany which came in an envelope addressed: 'Virginia Holgate, bronce-medal-gainer Los Angeles 1984, London.'

When we set off for Burghley, I was obviously hoping that the extreme lengths we had taken to accustom Night Cap to noisy crowds would pay dividends. But I was disappointed in his dressage, even though it was good enough to put us in fourth place after the first two days. I knew that he could have done better; he had again thrown marks away by being too tense and I felt exasperated with him. It seems such a waste of time and effort when a horse fails to perform to the best of its ability. I remember saying to Louise and Claire, who was still grooming for me, 'He'll never win a three-day event and he doesn't deserve to if he behaves like that.'

However, Night Cap went really well across country and we were in the lead before the final show jumping. As I warmed him up for that crucial final phase, I tried to pretend that I was cool and collected, that N's previous show jumping record at Burghley (one down in 1981 and two down the following year) had not in the least undermined my confidence. It was a delusion that was soon uncovered when I began jumping the practice fences. I could not, for the life of me, see a stride – which doesn't happen to me very often but, when it does, it's a nightmare.

Dot and Louise were with me out in the practice area as Night Cap jumped, either taking off from ridiculously far away or from the base of the fence. I could see them looking at each other as much as to say, 'What *are* we going to do with her?' However hard I tried, I simply could not get it right. Meanwhile my mother, racing between the collecting ring and the practice area, told us that time was running out.

Eventually Dot must have said to Louise, 'You'd better tell her everything's fine and we'll leave it at that.'

'I've seen you ride badly in your time, Ginny, but this is ridiculous,' said Louise, with a grin.

'I can't see a stride,' I told her.

'I'm not totally blind, I can see that for myself.' We looked at each other and we both started laughing.

'It's no good doing anything more, you'll just have to go in as you are,' said Louise, between giggles.

'Oh all right, that's what I'll do then.'

Had she been serious about my making a complete pig's ear of the practice fences, I would probably have gone to pieces. As it was, I rode into the arena feeling quite light-hearted and jumped the necessary clear round to win. I hasten to add that we rattled quite a few of the poles on the way, but we had threatened to do much worse than that. I have always reckoned that I owe my second Burghley win to Louise

121

and Dot's banter.

Towards the end of that month, I went to Portsmouth to take part in a television super-team challenge, promoted by Transworld International and sponsored by Townsend Thoresen. Our team of eight 'riders and drivers' which included cyclists, was to take on a 'stick and ball' side, which included some of the Olympic hockey players. Any idea that it was going to be a bit of crack, with no one caring too much as to which team won, was swiftly put aside. It was ferociously competitive from the moment we started on the first of our eight contests.

Show jumpers Steven Smith and Michael Whitaker, plus event rider Robert Lemieux, were on my team, and the four of us thought it was totally unfair that everyone, except us, would have the chance to compete once in something similar to their own sport. We would have liked to see some horses in the HMS Victory Arena, and we didn't waste any opportunity to say so. The first contest was a 1500 metre run in which I failed my team by finishing last. The winner had taken a shower and drunk a cup of coffee by the time I plodded home at the back of the field to sympathetic applause.

A cycle race followed and our coach, the ex-cycling star Hugh Porter, naturally left that to the non-horsey members of our team, who duly won. In the afternoon, we did a survival test. Four team members stayed on the docks holding a rope, while the rest of us leapt into the cold and murky water, swam to an upside-down life raft, turned it up the right way (Steven Smith's job), clambered in, tied one end of the rope to it, then let off a flare and unhitched the anchor (my task), before those on the dock pulled us in. The 'riders and drivers' won that too – we were looking good.

Last event of that day was the gym test, with its choice between bar jumps, press-ups, squat-thrusts or sit-ups. I was one of the four in our team to take part and I chose to do sit-ups (lying back, sitting up and touching knees with elbows) because it was the only one of the four exercises that seemed remotely possible. I did fifty-two within the time allowed of one minute and was totally exhausted – but we reckoned that the 'riders and drivers' were still doing well.

We slipped back the following day after losing the whaler race (possibly because I was cox!) and the tug o' war, which gave an easy victory to the much heavier 'stick and ball' team. We would have to make up lost ground in the deck hockey. I had played hockey at school, so I entered into it with a good deal of aggression and was livid when one chap on the opposing team tripped me up with his stick.

That might have been an accident, I thought, but knew that it wasn't when he tripped me up a second time. 'I'll get you,' I muttered, and gave him a quick whack on the shins!

Later in the game the same guy (who was over 6 feet tall) came up from behind, put his arms around me and held me in a vice-like grip so that I couldn't move. Suddenly claustrophobic, I yelled at him, 'Get your bloody arms off me.' Then, to my horror, I realised that there was a microphone just above my head; I had sworn on television! The big guy was sent off briefly for this foul and we won the deck hockey. Afterwards I went up to Emlyn Hughes, who was there to work on the television programme due out later that year. '*Please,*' I begged him, 'when you come to do the editing, would you *please* make sure that no one can hear what I was yelling?' Fortunately, the commentator talked over my words, which became a muffled sound of shouting, though he did say, 'She's getting a little irate!'

The two teams were level after we won the final obstacle contest and, much to our disgust, it was decided that a tug o' war would be used as the tie breaker. Steven Smith completely lost his cool on hearing this, as did a couple of the cyclists. I felt I had said enough for that day, so I sat looking meek and mild until we had to do the tug o' war, which inevitably went to our opponents.

I returned home, where we had a problem which seemed a minor one at the time. Priceless and Night Cap normally spend the winter months together out in the field but, while N was still in work, P had a different companion in Welton Elan. We had felt slight qualms about turning them out together and had had Welton Elan's hind shoes removed first – which was a fortunate precaution since one day, to our horror, he was seen to kick Priceless. There was no apparent damage and I therefore kept my engagement to ride P in the celebrity relay show jumping, against the clock, at the Horse of the Year Show in Wembley Arena.

I shudder every time I think what might have happened in that Wembley contest, because we later discovered that Priceless had a hair-line fracture just above the knee on the near fore. Concerned by the lump which had appeared, my mother contacted Don Attenburrow, who X-rayed the leg. Hair-line fractures don't necessarily show on an X-ray but, in this case, Don said there was a very definite indication that the bone had been cracked. This alarming discovery was made on 19 October and, from then until 11 December when he went down to Don's for a more thorough check, Priceless was more or less confined to his stable. He was led out very slowly four times a day to eat some grass, but we couldn't turn him loose for fear of the damage he might do to himself. Any sudden movement would have been liable to result in a severely broken leg.

It was while I was worrying myself sick about him that I had a phone call from Moysie Barton, our old friend from the Singapore days, who now lives near us at Shrewton. 'We're having some friends to lunch, so do come along and join us,' she said. I told her that Louise Bates was staying, so the invitation was extended to her as well.

For some reason, Batesy and I were feeling anti-social; we didn't feel like budging and it required a great effort of will-power to get changed and go out for lunch. Had we failed to do so, I would have missed the best prize of the year – Hamish Leng! I saw him for the first time as I walked in through Moysie's kitchen door: an amazing vision in morning suit, psychedelic shirt and bow tie, looking like someone who had just arrived from outer space instead of the house in the same village where his mother lives. To add to the bizarre scene, his two brothers, David and Adrian, were wearing pyjamas.

At 6 feet 4½ inches, Hamish is not easy to overlook even when he is more soberly dressed. Having taken a few furtive glances in the vision's direction, I decided he was actually very good looking and was rather peeved when he totally ignored me before lunch. During the meal, he sat next to me and I did my best to chat him up – but he seemed to be taking little notice of me. Right, I thought, two can play at that game, so I began chatting to everyone else at the table.

There had been no request for my telephone number or my address so I was surprised to receive a letter from Hamish about a week later. He said to give him a ring if I were ever in London, and he'd cook me a meal. Anxious not to seem too eager, I waited for a couple of weeks before phoning. 'I'm terribly sorry I haven't replied earlier, but I've been so booked up,' I said, attempting to give a totally false impression of my social life which had not, in fact, been all that hectic.

'Why don't you meet me for a drink and we'll go on somewhere afterwards?' said Hamish, suggesting a possible evening. I agreed to meet him at the Inn on the Park (which had already brought me some success in the past!) and was very impressed when I went in there to find him wearing his smart suit. I was equally impressed by the evening he had arranged; we went to the theatre to see *The Nerd*, dined out in a lovely restaurant and then went on to Annabel's to dance. I was delighted when he asked me if I would come to Shrewton the following weekend to meet his mother. Lady Leng (another Virginia) was in the middle of decorating when I arrived and I liked her instantly – much quicker, in fact, than I had liked her eldest son. Virginia and I have since become firm friends.

A few days later I flew out to New Zealand. The British Olympic team had been invited there to compete in an international three-day event on borrowed horses, and this time we managed to defeat the American gold medallists and win the team contest. I rode a smashing little 15.2 hh part-bred Arab, who slightly took the mickey out of me in the dressage, but was clear in both the cross-country and show jumping. Mark Phillips, taking the place of Lucinda, who was then pregnant, was the individual winner.

After winning the gold in Los Angeles (and the first equestrian medal of any colour to be won by a New Zealander) Mark Todd had become a national hero. When the television people decided to do their own version of *This is Your Life*, they chose him as their first subject. Karen Stives and I, having won the other two individual medals in LA, were asked to take part in the programme and we were both flown in a tiny plane to Wellington. Toddy, who thought he was being taken there for a straightforward interview, had left by plane about half an hour earlier.

We were smuggled into the Television Centre, into a room where his parents and friends were already hiding. When we started rehearsing for the programme, we had to be very careful how we crossed the corridor from the room to the studio: if Toddy were taking a stroll and happened to spot one of us, the gaff would be blown. It was all great fun and we achieved our aim by keeping Toddy in the dark; he had not the slightest suspicion about what lay ahead until the programme started and we began appearing on cue. He loved it – and so did those of us who were taking part.

I returned home to find Priceless much as I had left him. There was never any sign of lameness in the damaged foreleg, which we hoped was slowly healing. There was nothing we could do except keep him in, and pray. Meanwhile I was seeing a great deal more of Hamish Leng and keeping up the usual contact with Louise Bates, who became joint-master of the Pytchley Foxhounds in 1984.

Louise unwisely invited me to take Murphy Himself up for the Pytchley's opening meet. After two previous experiences, when she'd been forced to disown me, she should have known better. On one occasion I'd been with her to a very smart meet and was sitting quietly on my horse sipping sherry when the expensive glass slipped through my fingers and smashed on the gravel. Another time, when she had just become MFH, I went cubbing with her. I was on my horse, standing by the covert, as they began their calls of 'Ay-yi-yi Charley.'

Now I'll really embarrass her in front of her friends, I thought, unable to resist the temptation. 'Louise,' I said, in a stage whisper, 'why don't you call the fox Frederick?' She promptly blew a fuse, while her friends looked at me in some bewilderment, unable to decide whether this was a serious question or a joke.

When I accepted the invitation to the opening meet, I promised Louise that I would do my best to look respectable and to behave. I even had my hunting coat cleaned especially for the occasion. Unfortunately, the effect was spoilt when two buttons flew off it just before the meet and had to be replaced by safety pins. Murphy then proceeded to behave so badly that I was completely mortified; he leapt in the air, he ran away with me, he was a menace to everyone. By the end of the day, they had all had more than enough of the idiot rider with the safety pins, which may account for the fact that Louise has not asked me to hunt again.

Zimbabwe and Kenya were the next important entries in my diary. While I was in Los Angeles, I had met Elizabeth Warren-Codrington at one of the Horse Trials Support Group's parties and she had invited me to go to Zimbabwe, with a friend who could race ride, to take part in the first steeplechase to be held there for fifteen years. Naturally, I thought of my MFH mate. I don't think either Louise or I were wild about the idea of riding a borrowed horse in a three-mile 'chase, but the trip that was to follow it sounded far too good to miss, so I accepted the invitation for both of us.

Meanwhile Hamish, whom I had been seeing almost daily, had arranged to spend Christmas in Kenya and he invited me to fly on from Zimbabwe to join him there. That also sounded too good to miss. So I left poor Priceless with his injured leg, my poor mother, Dot and Elaine to cope with him, and flew off to enjoy myself.

Louise had probably anticipated some problem, since I was the person in charge of the arrangements for our trip to Zimbabwe, but the hitch at Harare Airport must still have come as a surprise. The immigration people needed to know where we would be staying and I couldn't for the life of me remember Mrs Warren-Codrington's address. We were told that we couldn't pass through customs and find the people who were due to meet us without producing this information.

Eventually I spotted two chaps through the glass, who looked as though they might be waiting for us, and I sent distress signals in their direction. Fortunately, the message was received and understood.

They managed to talk their way through the barrier that separated us and were able to give the necessary address. Our rescuers were Christopher Peach and Elizabeth Warren-Codrington's son, Bobby.

We were driven to the Oakley Equestrian Centre at Borrowdale where (as I should have remembered at Harare Airport) we were due to stay. Mrs Warren-Codrington greeted us, introduced us to the horses we would be riding and showed us round the course of beautifully built (but alarmingly substantial) fences that she had prepared. We had only a few days to get to know our mounts. Louise's Pergamena was a polo pony who had hardly ever jumped; my Son of Silver was a Thoroughbred who had done some show jumping but no racing. We both felt more than a little apprehensive as we thought about the task that lay ahead.

The night before the race was due to take place, we had three inches of rain and the meeting was cancelled. I hate to say it, but both Louise and I regarded this as a huge relief. The immediate future now looked far more enticing; Holiday Inns, who were sponsoring the race, had agreed to take us on a trip and we were certainly looking forward to that part of our stay. However, there was another hitch – the man who was organising the trip had gone abroad and no one else knew anything about it.

Once again Christopher Peach came to the rescue, contacting Geoff Hawkins of Holiday Inns who asked Robin Bailey to organise a trip for us. It began with a spectacular flight through the gorge of the Zambesi River to Victoria Falls. We travelled in the Holiday Inn's private plane with a marvellous pilot who flew low over the falls, giving us an incredible aerial view, before landing nearby. I took masses of photographs, including some magnificent shots without a film in the camera, which didn't surprise Louise in the least.

From Vic Falls we continued our journey in the private plane to stay at the Safari Lodge Hotel in the heart of the beautiful Whanki Game Reserve. That same night one of the game wardens ran into the hotel to say that our big chance to see some elephants had already arrived. Louise and I were among those who leapt into an open Land Rover to be driven down to the pan where the herd was drinking. To our utter amazement, we actually drove in amongst the herd of about fifty elephants, while the warden shone a spotlight on them. It was a stunning scene, but I don't think I have ever felt so vulnerable. In other words, I was absolutely petrified. One of the bulls seemed to be getting irate and it waved its trunk at us in what looked to Louise and me a very threatening manner. Its trunk was about two feet away from

127

Louise where she sat on the side of the open vehicle – and I am not allowed to repeat the comment she made as it moved away.

After a night in the hotel, we went to stay in Alan Elliott's tented camp for a few days, getting up early each morning to go out and look for wild animals. One evening we decided that we would like to search for lion – so, having warned us of the dangers, Alan Elliott led a group of us into the bush. We ate a marvellous stew, cooked on an open fire, and slept out in the open on mattresses. 'If there's a problem, just shout,' said Alan Elliott. 'I'll be here with my gun.'

'It won't be the lions that get us,' said a man from Scarborough, as he looked up to the trees that could be seen above our heads in the light of the fire. 'You mark my works, that blooming tree will fall down before the night's over.'

The mattresses had been laid out in a line and I found myself next to the Scarborough pessimist. Stupidly, I left my spare blanket on his feet and was frozen when I woke up in the night. So I grabbed the blanket, whereupon he leapt to his feet and started shouting, convinced that the lions had come to get us first after all. Alan Elliott was instantly awake with the gun in his hand; the rest of the party was in a state of frenzy, with everyone demanding to know what was happening. When the commontion died down, I was eventually able to explain all.

We were up very early that morning, this time according to plan, and we did have a thrilling view of a lioness. We also saw two rhinos at very close quarters and didn't much like the look of them. 'It's all right, Ginny,' said Louise, 'I'm right behind you!'

From there we travelled in canoes down the Zambesi River, on a three-day trip organised by John Rouse. We travelled light (taking no more than shorts, T-shirt, sweater and toothbrush) and were given just five minutes' instruction in our first-ever attempt at canoeing. 'There is only one rule,' we were told by Joe Rouse, John's brother, who was leading the trip. 'You must never get between a hippo and deep water, otherwise you're dead.' On that conforting note, we set forth.

Joe had no weapon of any kind as he led our little fleet down the Zambesi, banging the sides of his canoe so that any sleeping hippos would awaken and put their heads out of the water, letting us know their whereabouts. Since the river carried us along for much of the journey, we could enjoy the marvellous scenery without having to paddle furiously. The gentle movement was so relaxing that it was easy to forget the dangers and even Joe's concentration deserted him for a short while. He and the South African girl, who was sharing his canoe, were dozing when a hippo suddenly emerged from the water a few feet away from them and they almost capsized. After that terrifying moment, we all kept a sharp look out.

We spent three glorious days on the Zambesi, cooking on an open fire and sleeping out on its banks by night, swimming and washing in its waters, drifting or paddling down it by canoe. There was always a sense of danger, especially when waking in the middle of the night, without even a torch to guide you to a nearby bush. We had seen crocodiles as well as hippos, so were constantly aware that they were sharing this beautiful river with us. But it was a wonderful and unforgettable experience that both Louise and I will always cherish.

We went back to the Oakley Equestrian Centre at the end of our trip to find that the steeplechase had been postponed and not cancelled; it was due to take place shortly after our return. Our hopes were raised when the rain again fell in torrents on the night before the race, but this time they delayed making any decision until the course was inspected at 10 a.m. Louise and I suggested that, if they were to go ahead, our race should be run over one circuit instead of two because the ground was so deep. But it was to no avail; the meeting did take place and we were to do the full three miles. A certain amount of honour seemed to be at stake. Louise was a really good race rider and I was supposed to be able to pilot a horse across country – we would have to abandon thoughts of self-preservation and give it all we had. We neither disgraced ourselves nor broke our necks; Louise finished second to a jockey from Zimbabwe and I was third on the one and only ride I have ever had in a steeplechase, having survived a very near miss at the second last fence where I saw my horse's ears at close quarters.

We thanked Elizabeth Warren-Codrington for her marvellous hospitality and then went our separate ways; Louise flew back home to resume her important role with the Pytchley while I stayed a couple of days with Christopher Peach and his family before flying to Kenya for my date with Hamish. A nasty thought crossed my mind as the plane came to a halt in Nairobi Airport: what on earth will I do if Hamish doesn't turn up? But I need not have worried. He and his brother, Adrian, were there to meet me and to drive me north into the mountains at Molo where we stayed with their friends, Michael and Jean Skinner.

Michael Skinner took us on a super four-day trip to a tented camp in the Masai Mara District, where we looked at wild animals in the morning and lazed around for the rest of the day. Then we returned to the Skinners' lovely old house at Molo for Christmas.

'Look at me,' said Hamish, while I was wrapping parcels late on Christmas Eve after the others had all gone to bed. As soon as he had spoken, the lights went out.

'Oh sure, I'm looking,' I laughed, as we stood in the dark.

'Will you marry me?' asked Hamish.

I was so taken by surprise that he had to repeat the question.

'Yes, of course I will,' I said.

I had absolutely no idea that he was going to ask me but, since I was already dotty about him, I didn't need to waste any time in making up my mind. We agreed that this would remain our secret over Christmas and the New Year, then we would tell our families before anyone else. Meanwhile we had a wonderful Christmas, complete with roast turkey and log fires, before moving down to the coast at Kilifi, near Mombasa, to stay in the Skinners' all-white and stunningly beautiful seaside house. We swam and sailed; we went fishing and ski-ing; we lazed in the sun and feasted ourselves on mangoes, prawns and other delicacies. Many miles away in England the horses were plodding along the roads in the raw cold of January, getting fit for the 1985 eventing season.

THIRTEEN
A Priceless Badminton

Our vet, Don Attenburrow, is inclined to play down the enormous contribution he has made towards the success of our horses; he insists that my mother deserves the recognition. 'It's her restless nature, her attention to detail and determination to make things work that is more important,' he says.

My mother tends to challenge everything he tells her. 'She's bright and eager to learn,' according to Don, 'and that works better. If someone sits and takes everything you say as though you're the Archangel Gabriel, it even becomes boring for the Archangel.'

So the discussions concerning Priceless, and whether or not he should compete in the spring events of 1985, were by no means one-sided. I have far less contact with Don than my mother does, but I also like to hear him explain each situation so that I can be convinced we are doing the right thing.

The first important decision had to be taken while I was still away. Priceless was to have some slow ridden work, for ten days in the arena and then on the roads, to start getting fit again. He had done some trotting before a second X-ray was taken on 30 January, which seemed to show satisfactory healing. He did one show jumping competition at Crookham before he went back to Don's place near Exeter for a second 'scan' on 12 March.

Don, who is a Research Fellow in the Medical Physics group in the Physics Department of Exeter University, has adapted a method well established in human medicine to investigate bone diseases and injuries in animals. It is called scintigraphy and has been used in humans for many years. Apparently bone is not the solid, unchanging thing that most of us imagine. 'It is constantly changing to cope with the stresses that are put on it,' says Don, 'and the reason it is able to respond is because it has a tremendous blood supply.'

Don's scintigraphy is a means of locating abnormal bone activity (in other words, the place where the bone is reacting to either injury or disease) by finding out where there is a larger than normal blood supply. He does this by injecting the horse with a special chemical to which radio-active isotopes are attached. This particular chemical makes straight for the bones, taking the isotopes with it, and concentrates in those areas where the blood supply is greatest.

The amount of radiation is insignificant and harmless, while the readings from Don's hand-held scanner (taken about twelve hours after the injection) are marvellously informative. When he did the first 'scan' on Priceless in December 1984 he compared the readings on the damaged near-fore with those on the off-fore; the difference between the two then suggested that the cracked bone had not yet finished healing. In March, the readings were close enough to indicate (far more conclusively than an X-ray could) that the bone had mended.

So we asked Don whether P should go to Badminton. As he has said since, 'The decision was made as a result of discussion; I advise people, I don't direct them. We knew that the lump had resolved itself and the horse was sound, so we used scintigraphy – as well as common sense – to assist us in making that decision.'

Don has to have a Department of the Environment licence to practice scintigraphy and his is the only practice in Europe that offers such a service. He also has a sophisticated research laboratory which he uses for diagnosing the problems in horses sent to him through his veterinary practice. Priceless had to stay with him for the regulation forty-eight hours before he came back to us and, having made the decision to take him to Badminton, he resumed his training, which was now behind schedule. The British team vet, Peter Scott-Dunn, had already been informed about what was happening, so the selectors were kept in the picture.

Our next problem was caused by the weather. I normally take the horses to Wylye, for a cross-country school with Lady Hugh, before riding them in their first one-day event of the season. This time every appointment that was made had to be cancelled because of snow. When I took Priceless and Night Cap ('the boys' as I often call them) to Rushall for the advanced section, I hadn't jumped a single cross-country fence on P since the Olympics, or with N since Burghley.

I was feeling distinctly nervous without that preliminary school, which normally helps to get rid of the cobwebs, but I was really thrilled with the way they both went. Night Cap doesn't squander his talent at one-day events, where there are no big crowds to distract him; he was leading at the end of the dressage and went on to win, with Priceless second. The following weekend 'the boys' ran at Brigstock, where they won two of the three advanced sections. The other one went to Mark Todd and his Olympic gold medal partner, Charisma.

So my first journeys in the smart new cream and brown lorry supplied by British National Life Assurance, who were now my sponsors, had been thoroughly worthwhile. But the big goal was Badminton, with its cross-country phase three weeks after Brigstock, and the intervening time between competitions left me with my usual itchy feet. Karen Stives, a firm friend since we both took part in Mark Todd's *This is Your Life*, had come over from the States with her Olympic horse, Ben Arthur, and was staying with me while she competed at Badminton. When she went off to ride at Belton a week after Brigstock, my feet became even more itchy.

Those final weeks leading up to Badminton are not the best time of the year to have anyone to stay. I was anxious in case Karen might find our facilities inadequate, that she would be worried because there are no hills in our part of the world that she could use to build up her horse's fitness. But she was fabulous; it would be impossible to have anyone easier to stay during the final preparation for Badminton and the event itself.

Those of us who were getting two horses ready were faced with a late threat of having to withdraw one of them because of the huge number of entries. Fortunately, enough people pulled out during the last few weeks to bring the field down to manageable proportions; it would have been terribly frustrating to leave one horse in his stable after the months of preparation.

My 'boys' were incredibly fit. The new training schedule, worked out the previous summer, is used after I have brought them to one-day event fitness by the old method of interval training. After that I move on to short, sharp work and I have found that they are not only much fitter as a result, but are mentally much happier as well. They felt as ready as they could ever be for the big test when I travelled up to London to face my first challenge of Badminton week. Three days before the dressage started, I was to appear on the Terry Wogan show.

I met Louise for some shopping in London before the programme and, I'm afraid, failed to show the thrift implicit in Grandpa's favourite saying (which my mother has often quoted to me since his death), 'A man's wealth lies not in the abundance of his riches, but in the fewness of his wants.' Having spent too much money, I dragged Louise with me to the television studio.

We were given our own dressing room, which made us feel very important. I then had to go to the make-up room, where all my own efforts in front of the mirror were completely removed and they started again from scratch. During this long process, Terry Wogan looked in for a quick chat – without revealing any of the questions he would be putting to me in front of the cameras. Back in the dressing room, I asked the research lady if she could give me any clue as to the questions I would have to answer. 'Absolutely not,' she said. 'If I did that, it wouldn't be spontaneous.'

Louise and I watched the guests before me from a glass area above the studio; by now I was feeling really nervous and was convinced that I would fall up the step and go sprawling across the studio floor. I was taken downstairs four minutes before I was due to appear and they counted me down from two minutes, which was distinctly nerve-racking. 'Don't worry, you'll be all right. Just remember that you're a woman and you're looking very pretty,' someone said to me shortly before I was due to go on. I can't say that was much help. I was more concerned about negotiating the step and about how I should sit – with legs crossed or uncrossed, sitting up or leaning back, hands on my lap or wherever. I was also worrying about my spontaneous answers to those unknown questions; since it was going out live, I couldn't afford to make a blunder.

By some miracle, I got up the step safely and managed to talk without too much of a quiver in my voice. The most difficult question was when Terry Wogan put on a toffee-nosed accent and asked, 'Why is it that all the riders speak like this?' There was a split-second of near panic before I answered him in my best Cockney accent, 'Well, if you want me to, I'll speak like that.' Most of the time we talked about horses and the week's big event at Badminton, which was much easier to manage.

We were given a drink when the show was over; Terry Wogan joined us, looking very relaxed, and chatted away with tremendous charm. Having dolled ourselves up for the occasion, Louise and I then found ourselves at a loose end for the rest of the evening. We were both ravenous, so we went to the nearest place we could find and ate hamburgers, looking ridiculously overdressed among the jeans and T-shirts.

Two days later, I had my first walk round the 1985 Badminton cross-country course. Among the thirty-three fences there were two that really worried me – Fairbanks Bounce (a sheer drop followed by rails) and the lake (with its double of rails going into the water). Both involved a bounce if you went the fast route and I knew how easy it would be to get them wrong. I asked Lady Hugh for her advice.

'You go the fast way at every fence with Priceless,' she said, with Dot in full agreement. She has tremendous respect for P's intelligence and has often suggested that I should pin the cross-country map on the wall of his stable and leave the rest to him. Earlier in the year, she had told me that I must be sure to run him at Badminton because she had a funny feeling he was going to win.

'No,' I had said, 'he'll never win Badminton.'

'Just you make sure you take him there,' was her reply.

So here I was, with two horses and a couple of extremely worrying cross-country fences to ponder over. I had chosen to ride Night Cap first because he would then do his dressage in the morning, while there were fewer people around to distract him. Even so, the atmosphere would be highly charged compared with a one-day event and we had to think of the best means possible of ensuring that he wouldn't light up as soon as he entered the arena. This time we decided to keep him near the arena, that we wouldn't take him away from the collecting ring area as we had in the past.

He was worked on the lunge for about forty minutes, then I rode him for half an hour. After that we removed his tack, put a cavesson on him and he was allowed to eat grass in the collecting ring, where he could hear the noise of people clapping. I then went off to get changed and, when I came back, we tacked him up again so that I could work him in for forty minutes before doing my test. This new ploy really seemed to work. Night Cap's test was one of the best he has ever done; he was lying in fourth place and leading the British entries when the two days of dressage were completed. Priceless, who loves performing in front of a big crowd, was in sixth place.

Alone in the bungalow that evening, I began to panic as I went through the cross-country fences in my head. It was a welcome relief when Hamish turned up, fresh from his week's ski-ing holiday. He put his arms round me and told me that Big Gin of Ivyleaze would be all right on the day.

There was a minor problem the following day when Night Cap lost a shoe on the steeplechase course but Robert Hall, our farrier, was there to tap another one on quickly while I looked around to see where my mother had parked. I knew that Dot would be stationed in front of the closed-circuit television, so that she could give me last-minute information before I rode the cross-country, but my mother, Uncle Jack, Hamish and Elaine had intended to drive out to the steeplechase. Suddenly the four appeared, red in the face like unfit joggers, with their arms full of rugs and buckets. My mother was livid because the car had broken down; they'd had to abandon it and run to the steeplechase course over a distance which tends to vary according to which of the four is relating the story. The details, relayed by Mummy as she towel-dried Night Cap, were punctuated by her low opinion of a certain make of car, which I dare not name.

N's shoe was tapped on lightly before I rode the second section of roads and tracks, then secured more firmly during the ten-minute halt. My confidence was given a wonderful boost when he went clear over the cross-country course, taking the fast route through both of the fences that had worried me to finish with just 4 time penalties. Having completed the course on my first horse, I went off to the lorry on my own to sit and think.

First I had to eat something, so I forced down a Kit-Kat (thinking that I never wanted to look at one again) and drank a cup of coffee. Then I ran through my entire round on Night Cap in my head, before going through the whole journey again while I imagined myself on Priceless. When this mental process was over, it was virtually time to get on P and put thoughts into action. Despite the confidence that N had given me, I was still fraught with anxiety as I set out for my second 15-mile ride.

There was a snowstorm when I rode the steeplechase course on Priceless and I could scarcely see a thing. Any minute now, I thought, we're going to gallop into one of the fences. I was so blinded by the snow that was flying into our faces, it seemed impossible that P would be able to see enough to jump them. I felt a huge sense of relief when we finished safely and within the optimum. Riding through the now wintry landscape on the next stage of roads and tracks, I prayed that the sun would come out and that we would complete the rest of our journey without my making any blunders.

The snow eased off and eventually stopped while P's familiar and seemingly lethargic trot carried us to the Box for the ten-minute halt. Once there he stood quite still, looking thoroughly dopey, waiting for the usual preparations to be made before he went across country. When Elaine, his groom, went to lead him towards the start, there was none of the excited jigging about that you see in most horses. Priceless was reluctant to move and, when he eventually did so, he walked forward in a dull slouch. Having conserved his energy with an intelligence that is almost uncanny, he went completely berserk as I prepared to get on him. Once I was aboard, he did his imitation of a Spanish Riding School horse with 'airs above the ground' that resembled capriole and levade. There were three people holding his bridle while Elaine struggled to tighten his girth and I was delighted when the starter's countdown ended with the welcome word, 'Go.'

A branch caught the side of my face and cut it as I jumped through the trees at Huntsman's Leap (fence four) and I had to make a conscious effort to forget about that while I concentrated on the job in hand. Having done so, I had one of those magical rides that you rarely (if ever) experience. Priceless is like a machine to ride across country; all I needed to do was point him towards a fence and set him up for it; he did the rest. He was so wonderfully fit and well that he felt as fresh at the end of the course as he had when setting out, and we finished well within the optimum time.

At the end of the day, Mark Todd was leading on Charisma, from America's Torrance Watkins-Fleischmann on Finvarra; I was third on Priceless and fourth on Night Cap. Between the two of us, Torrance and I would make a pretty good bionic woman, since she had her right arm re-assembled in the January of 1977 and it is now held together by two plates and forty-eight screws. Amputation was also considered in her case, which was considerably worse than mine, with a fractured skull among the injuries inflicted by a devastating kick from a horse she was leading.

Both Torrance and I were within 5 penalties of Mark Todd as we warmed up for the final show jumping, knowing that a single error could be very costly. Night Cap, just over 5 penalties behind Toddy's Charisma, went earlier than his normal place on the reverse order of merit so that I would have time to switch to Priceless without holding up the action that was being transmitted on television. N jumped a super clear round and that was a big thrill; he rarely touches anything with his forelegs, but does have a tendency to let one hindleg trail and have a fence down.

That's wonderful, I thought, Mr N is going to be fourth. Now for Priceless. Out in the collecting ring, P was jumping out of his skin over the practice fences. Normally he touches one and then sharpens up, but this time he was really ballooning. Knowing how much was at stake, I felt ill as I rode into the arena — and ecstatic when I rode out having jumped a clear round.

Dorothy put her arm round me after I had dismounted and said, 'The other two have to jump the clear rounds now, you know.'

I looked at her, well aware of the implication behind her words. 'No,' I told her, 'it will never happen.'

I was outside, patting Priceless, when I heard a great roar from the crowd. 'Whatever's happened?' I asked, and was told that Torrance had just hit two parts of the treble.

Mark Todd then disappeared from my view as he rode into the arena. I was still patting Priceless when I heard an enormous cheer from the grandstands. So Mark's won, I thought, and turned towards the exit from the arena in order to congratulate him as he rode out. Meanwhile I saw Hamish running towards me. 'Mark's had a fence down,' he said.

'What do you mean?' I asked. 'He can't have had a fence down.'

'Well he has – and you've won.' I looked at Hamish as the words sank in and then burst into tears!

I was first on Priceless and third on Night Cap, with Mark Todd second and Torrance Watkins-Fleischmann fourth.

Roger Davies, managing director of British National Life Assurance, hadn't for a moment thought that I would win and that he would be walking into the area to meet the Queen. He looked down in distress at his welly boots and said to my mother, 'I can't possibly go in like this, you'll have to go in instead of me.'

There was an argument that lasted about five minutes, before Roger was persuaded to receive the Whitbread Trophy in his wellies. He managed the whole thing rather better than I did. I rode in and, typically, got off the horse at the wrong time. I then had to remount and wait until I was told to get off. Having dismounted for the second time, I walked up to the Queen and gave a small curtsy – after which, I'm afraid, Her Majesty didn't have much of a chance to get a word in edgeways. In the excitement of the moment, I was quite unable to stop jabbering. 'Isn't it wonderful that the weather stayed fine?' I said. 'I do hope you didn't get too cold watching the show jumping – and did you find it exciting?' Eventually, as I paused for breath, she managed to congratulate me!

Hamish very sweetly went off to buy champagne, which we drank during a marvellous party at home that night. Michael and Jean Skinner, who had flown all the way from Kenya to watch Badminton, joined us for the celebrations and most of the riders we had invited called in on their way home. It was after ten o'clock before I managed to change out of my riding clothes.

A couple of days later, still mesmerised by the happenings at Badminton, I rode in the Farriers Invitation Private Stakes over the Derby course at Epsom. Among the sixteen of us who had been invited to ride in the race were Princess Anne, Malcolm Wallace, Maureen Piggott (daughter of Lester), Joanna Winter (daughter of Fred) and the eventual winner, Elaine Mellor. Since the purpose of the exercise was to raise money for Riding for the Disabled we were all sponsored – in my case by the estate agents, Hampton and Sons. I met my mount, Taras Chariot (trained by Philip Mitchell) for the first time when I arrived at Epsom. Because of Badminton, there had been no opportunity to accept Jeremy Tree's kind offer to ride out with his string of racehorses, so my first experience of short stirrups was when riding down to the start of the race itself and I found it quite extraordinary – even though I wasn't riding nearly as short as Princess Anne, who finished fourth, quite a few places ahead of me.

No one had thought to warn me that after riding with the stirrups so short, your legs tend to give way when you dismount. I now realise why you often see a trainer waiting for the jockey to get off and then holding him for a second or two. I got off and collapsed in a heap, before Hamish picked me up and drove me home.

While I was out, my mother had received a phone call from Graham Kimberley, sales manager of Charles Follett Ltd in London. 'Would you like a car?' he asked.

Thinking it was a joke, she said, 'Well, it depends what kind.'

'How would you like a Porsche?'

'Oh, how lovely, I'll have two or three.' There was a silence at the end of the phone, before my mother added, 'Was there anything else?'

'I am serious, you know. I think I ought to come and see you,' said Graham. So he was given directions on how to get to Ivyleaze and that, thought my mother, would be the end of it.

When I came home she told me, almost in passing, that some chap had phoned up and talked about giving me a Porsche, but she wasn't expecting anything to come of it. To our amazement he turned up. I treated his arrival fairly casually, unable to believe in this story of a car that would be ours to drive for a year, and left him to talk with my mother. She, too, was full of doubts. 'Nobody gets anything for nothing,' she said, 'and I don't see what Ginny can possibly do in return.'

Apparently all they wanted was for me to drive one of the new C-registration Porsches that were due out shortly (and which would have my name and Charles Follett's on the side of it) and attend a few functions. It was understood that my programme was far too hectic for me to commit myself to making more than a few appearances during the year, so we happily accepted the car which is one of the best things we've ever done. Not only do we love the car, but Graham Kimberley and the whole firm are delightful and great fun.

One of the functions was a day at Brands Hatch for those of Charles

Follett's customers who owned Porsches. Hamish came with me and we were instructed by Formula One drivers amid much smoke and squealing of tyres. Eventually, I was allowed to sit in the passenger seat, while a racing driver took me round the track at full speed, which was a terrifying experience. We then swapped places and I frightened myself some more by whizzing round, doing my level best to follow his instructions. That evening I felt more exhausted than I had after riding two horses in the speed, endurance and cross-country phase at Badminton.

FOURTEEN
Going for gold

'You now have the harmony,' Dot said to me as I started my preparations for the 1985 European Championships at Burghley. 'When I watched you at Badminton, I could see that you had finally achieved the harmony and the confidence between yourself and the two horses that you've always been aiming for. Now you must keep it, you mustn't allow any self-doubt back in your mind.'

I hoped that I could follow her advice, not only for my own sake but also for the great team working at home. Apart from my mother and Dot, there were Elaine Pickworth, who looks after Priceless, and Nicki Ide-Smith, who takes care of Night Cap and Murphy Himself. Both had come to us as working pupils and asked to stay on after the normal one year was completed. There were also Wendy Tyrell and Nicky Fleming, who were looking after two of our five-year-olds and the youngsters.

P's groom, Elaine, is the only working pupil who has competed on one of our horses. She had shown talent as a rider and we wanted to give her the chance to compete, so she rode a five-year-old called Bally McGinty in one-day events and hunter trials during 1985 and did well on him before the horse was eventually sold.

Maita Robinson, who helps with the massive amount of paperwork and the accounts, is another important part of the team. Her husband Robby, who is an RAF pilot, has his own video camera and he has been marvellous at coming to events and recording our efforts, giving me the chance to watch myself with a critical eye.

One of our biggest headaches involves planning the schedule for the spring and autumn seasons, which Maita and I do together. Before I ride the baby novices in events, I have to work out when I can canter the big boys that are being prepared for a full-scale three-day test. I do all the fast work with the advanced horses while they are getting fit, and dove-tailing their programme in with the ones lined up for the youngsters is a real juggling act. Everything has to be recorded in the diary so that entry forms can be sent off to arrive before the closing date. We also have dates to arrange for the lecture/demonstrations that I am asked to give and a constant flow of correspondence to answer.

Everything was (we hoped) under control when the 1985 autumn season got under way. I made a long, but thoroughly satisfying trip to the Holker Hall one-day event in Cumbria where Night Cap won the Advanced Section and Priceless was fourth. Ian Stark won practically everything else, with a total of four wins (which included beating me into second place on Murphy Himself in the Open Intermediate) as well as taking second and third in the Advanced. A month later, N and P finished first and second in the Midland Bank Advanced Championships at Locko Park, which again incorporated the final trial for the European Championships. So far the harmony seemed to be holding out!

Hamish had turned up unexpectedly at Locko when I was walking the course for the show jumping. It was a lovely surprise because he'd promised to play in a cricket match and I had assumed he wouldn't be there. Poor Hamish, who has a demanding business life as a financial adviser, seemed to have spent most of his leisure hours during 1985 revolving his life around mine – and I felt quite guilty because I didn't seem able to put myself out for him. If he were invited to bring me to a party, I invariably had to decline because it clashed with an event.

For someone who likes to be active, it must have been a bore for him to go through the inevitable hanging around while I was busy with the horses. 'I love the sport and watching you,' he would say, 'but I feel so useless.' He may in the future become more actively involved in the team – walking the horse round, hosing it down or whatever – but he has always done a tremendous amount for me just by being there.

Four days after Locko I had a fall that resulted in a hair-line fracture in my left wrist. I was riding another of Ben Faerie's sons, the then five-year-old Beneficial, in a novice event at Windsor Park. We had come flying through the finish only to find our path blocked. The right-hand route that I had intended to take was now full of people, so I swung left only to find some vehicles parked in my way. There was no alternative but to go straight on across the rope and, having failed to see it until the last moment, poor Beneficial was tipped over onto a gravel path. He was a very sorry sight, with cuts on both knees and on his nose, and I knew he wouldn't event again that year. I could only hope that the incident would not leave a psychological scar as well.

I was taken off to St Margaret's Hospital, near Windsor, where I learnt about the hair-line fracture. My left wrist was protected by a splint when I rode Murphy three days later at Iping, where Lucinda Green had a fall and damaged some ligaments in her right shoulder. The British European Championships team was scarcely looking in great shape!

In my usual anxious way, I wanted to ride in one more contest before the European Championships, otherwise there would have been a long gap between competitions during which any doubts about my riding were likely to be magnified. I was therefore keen to take Night Cap to the Scottish Championships at Thirlestone. Henrietta Knight, Chairman of the Selection Committee, said she would prefer me not to go. 'If you still decide to go, that's fine,' she said, 'but I wanted you to know that the Committee would prefer you to forget about Thirlestone.'

Hen has always been wonderfully approachable and I was very grateful when she left the final decision to me. There was much humming and hawing at home before I decided to make that long journey in the horsebox to Scotland, but I was delighted that I had done so after Night Cap won and my cross-country riding felt reasonably fluent.

That amazing Yorkie Bar Kid (my mother) drove the lorry the whole way home while I had a lift with Richard Meade. We stopped for dinner en route and I treated Richard, Angela (known to everyone as Tiddles) and Mary Gordon-Watson to a cold and greasy hamburger. I suppose it's the thought that counts! My return by car brought me home in time for some frenzied packing as we were due at Wylye for team training the following day.

Meanwhile, we had all been distressed to learn that Lord and Lady Hugh Russell were being forced to sell their lovely Bathampton House together with all the wonderful facilities they have provided for us over the years at Wylye. Their place was not only the best training centre for three-day eventers in Britain, it was also the best in the world. In the realisation of how much those facilities would be missed, I also had to appreciate my great good fortune in being able to use them for so many years. Needless to say, those of us who have trained together there for major championships were also aware of how much we would miss the wonderful hospitality.

While in training for Burghley, I was chosen to ride Priceless in the European Championships team with Lucinda Green on Regal Realm, Ian Stark on Oxford Blue and Rodney Powell on Pomeroy. Lorna Clarke, Clarissa Strachan and Madeleine Gurdon, who joined us for the Wylye training, would be competing as individuals unless anyone on the team had a problem and needed to be replaced. All seven of us, plus our new chef d'équipe Lord Patrick Beresford, put on the smart outfits that had been kindly provided by Simpsons, to have our photograph taken together at Wylye. Shortly afterwards, poor Rodney Powell had to withdraw because of problems with his horse, Pomeroy, and Lorna Clarke was brought onto the team in his place with Myross.

Following in the footsteps of Malcolm Wallace cannot have been easy for Patrick, but he was terrific. Wol had reluctantly given up as chef after becoming Director-General of the British Equestrian Federation and, in fact, had a big role to play in the European Championships when standing in as substitute Director for Charles Stratton, who was sadly unable to be there because of illness. We sent Charles some flowers from Priceless and had a marvellous letter from Ann Stratton immediately after the Championships. 'Dear Priceless,' it began, 'As Charles has not yet passed the vet, I am writing to thank you . . .'

When it came to deciding the team order, Lucinda insisted on going first. 'I was the one who was least on form,' she said, at one of the press conferences, 'so it was obviously right that I should go first.' The rest of us were grateful; it meant that we would have marvellously explicit information on the fences that worried us most; we knew we could rely on her to be a magnificent path-finder. Lorna Clarke was to go second for the team, with Ian Stark third. I would be fourth and last, which was splendid except for the fact that I would have to wait, feeling sick with apprehension, while the other three went before me!

We stayed with Joss and Rosy Hanbury, who had generously included Hamish among the guests at their spectacular Burley-on-the-Hill home, and we couldn't have found a happier base from which to try and recapture the European team title. I'd been given such a wonderful year that I felt the only possible return I could make for my good fortune was by doing my utmost to be a good team member.

Some daunting fences were waiting to be inspected on the first walk round. The Bullfinch (fence 4) seemed enormous; both Trout Hatchery obstacles (fences 5 and 25/6) looked as though they were liable to cause plenty of trouble with their jumps into water. In my case, there was another problem in Priceless's sudden aversion to the flies and midges that were around in great abundance that autumn, after endless weeks of rain. He began flicking his head against them and I was concerned that he might ruin his dressage by doing this throughout his test. Because he was feeling so incredibly fit, I was also worried in case his test might be spoilt by an exuberant buck or two, which has happened in the past.

Having discussed this possibility with Dot, it was decided that I should give him his pipe-opening gallop on the morning of his dressage, so that he could let off a bit of excess steam. He had a short couple of bursts up a steep hill and was then returned to his stable. I didn't do any flat work on him that day until the normal hour's warm-up before we were due into the dressage arena, where he would have achieved by far the best test of his life had it not been for two halts at which he refused to stand still. Even so, the quality of his work was so far superior to anything I'd experienced before that I had to be thrilled with him. His trot was so much more engaged and light that I suppose something had to give, especially as he was fitter then he's ever been in his life.

P's score of 49 penalties left me ninth of the 59 riders at the end of the dressage, with the Belgian, Raf de Smedt, well out in front on 35.8 until he withdrew Urs the following day. Our best rider at that stage was Madeleine Gurdon, one of the seven British individuals competing, who was seventh on a score of 48 with her marvellous The Done Thing. Dusty, as her horse is otherwise known, is the same height as Priceless at 16 hh and he is built on similar lines, which gives me a special affection for him. Sadly, his chance of a medal was to end with an unlucky fall on the steeplechase course.

Germany was leading the nine teams with Britain second when the dressage ended. While those scores were being worked out, I went through about three hours of interviews – with press, radio and television – and was grateful that I had walked the course earlier in the day. Anything that is good for the sport is obviously worth doing, but it was a relief when all the talking ended and I was at last able to get out of my dressage coat and relax.

As I was going last for the team, I had the opportunity of watching the earlier riders on closed-circuit television as they tackled the 30 cross-country fences. I had already discussed the various routes at great length with my mother and Dot. Watching seemed a dubious advantage after the first 15 horses had graphically illustrated the problems I was about to face and seriously lowered my morale in the process. Eight of those first 15 had falls and three others were eliminated. There had been one clear round, in a slow time, from the Frenchman Jean Teulere and a single refusal from Lucinda Green on Regal Realm, which was a depressing sight for me because they are both so brilliant across country. Had Lucinda gone later, with the

145

benefit of all the information that our wonderful band of helpers brought back to the Box, she would undoubtedly have taken a different route at Capability's Cutting and avoided that one mistake.

Lorna Clarke and Myross, the sixteenth horse to go, then jumped a magnificent clear round, overtaking the Italian rider who had started four minutes before her. While he was taking the slow serpentine route through the Upper Trout Hatchery, Lorna came storming past on the direct straight line, making it look wonderfully easy. I felt much better after watching her round and decided not to look at any more! It proved to be a sensible decision as far as my morale was concerned because the eight horses that followed Myross either fell or were eliminated.

It is my custom to wear odd socks on cross-country day. This daft bit of superstition goes back to my junior days when I rarely seemed able to find a matching pair. After winning the Junior European Championships, I had discovered that I was wearing one blue and one red sock. So it became crystal clear that odd socks were lucky! I never wear green, because that would be unlucky – not that I know this from personal experience, I have never dared to risk it! Suitably attired, I completed the two sections of roads and tracks and the steeplechase course without any problem to arrive at the Box, where good news awaited me. Ian Stark had gone fast and clear on Oxford Blue and our team was already well in the lead.

'The team's in good shape,' said Patrick Beresford, 'so you go on the routes you want to take.'

Having planned my whole approach around the team effort, I had to think quickly. Some of the fast routes, in particular the corner at the Maltings Wall, had caused problems and I was expecting to be told that I should take the longer routes at certain obstacles; my mind was already geared to following this anticipated instruction. But now I had been offered the chance to ride for an individual medal and, while I was on Priceless and waiting to start, I was still asking myself: 'Shall I go for the corners after all?'

I looked down at Lucinda, who was standing by Ian and waiting to see me off. She must have been reading my mind, because she looked up at me and said: 'Go for gold.' Those three unforgettable words swept all indecision aside and gave me the confidence I needed.

Priceless slightly worried me for the first twelve fences. He was jumping beautifully and going fast enough, but he wasn't pulling in his normal way and I kept thinking: why isn't he taking hold? I used my legs on him as we were on our way towards the massive Bullfinch

146

at fence 4 and he gave a buck. The message was clear enough; I was to belt up and leave him alone, he was the one in charge. I never touch him with a stick, except to give him one tap on the shoulder if we're coming into a difficult combination or a line on which we need to stay very straight. He doesn't mind that single tap because he understands the message that it's supposed to convey – but, if I were to try touching him behind the saddle, he would certainly retaliate with unwanted vigour.

The crowd around the dreaded Bullfinch let out a tremendous cheer as Priceless sailed over it, which gave my spirits a real lift and made me feel much braver! I have never experienced such enthusiastic crowds before; like the rest of my team-mates, I heard loud cheering every time P cleared one of the more difficult fences and it was wonderfully elating. After bouncing through the Rotunda at fence 12, we made a turn that left us pointing for home and, from there until the end of the course, Priceless took hold and pulled like a train!

His jumping – through all the fast routes, including the difficult corner at the Maltings Wall – was brilliant and almost nonchalant; none of the fences that had caused so many problems to the other horses caused him the slightest concern. As usual, all I had to do was set him up for each fence and point him in the right direction. Priceless was the only horse to finish within the optimum time and I was leading at the end of the day, with the British team now a distance ahead of France and Germany.

That evening, the Holgate team had dinner with our sponsors. 'Anything can happen,' I warned them, only too well aware that the one show jumping fence I had in hand was not enough to ensure the individual gold medal, although the team was fortunately in good shape.

'It doesn't matter,' they said. 'Whatever you do tomorrow, we're still proud of you.' Those were among the nicest words I have ever heard.

Another long and fraught afternoon was in store while I waited to do my show jumping last, in the usual reverse order of merit. Ian Stark's one mistake on Oxford Blue gave me a second fence in hand as I rode into the arena, but I still felt terribly nervous. Meanwhile, Priceless had summed up the importance of the occasion in his usual way and, having pinged clear over the practice fences, he did the same in the arena where it mattered most. I had won the individual gold, with Lorna Clarke moving up to take the silver and Ian Stark winning the bronze. Young Mandy Orchard, riding as one of our individuals was fourth on Venture Busby and Lucinda finished sixth on Regal Realm. As Patrick Beresford said at the ensuing press conference, the British victory had been so overwhelming that it was almost an embarrassment. 'But,' he added, 'it's an embarrassment that I'm prepared to live with!'

The most thrilling moment for me was riding in with my team-mates to receive our gold medals. There had been a wonderful feeling of comradeship between us; that sense of shared achievement and total loyalty seemed to unite us in a special way as we went in together for the presentation. I have been on some marvellous teams, but this one seemed the best of all. Our subsequent celebrations began in the Remy Martin tent and continued in the stable area, where I was lucky enough to escape the usual immersion in the water trough and my only discomfort came later with a mild dose of too-much-champagne! During the party my mother, Dot and I sneaked off to see Priceless, who wondered what the silly fuss was all about.

British National Life Assurance had been running a competition that summer among its twenty branch offices, with the offer of a free trip to Burghley for those who won. When the Coventry branch came out on top, the winners had generously asked that the money should be given to charity and it was therefore decided that Riding for the Disabled would be the appropriate beneficiary. To my great delight, it was then agreed that Pat Burgess should use it to buy another horse for her marvellous RDA Group and, by way of doubling my pleasure in that decision, my sponsors said that they would celebrate my victory by increasing the amount to cover the cost of two horses. Pat had never come to a European Championship before, but she was at Burghley to see her team win. She was also celebrating with us in the stables when Roger Davies told us of the gift that his firm would be making. It was a great joy for me because it meant that my win had brought some return to Pat, who had helped me so much.

Back at home, Priceless began his slow wind down to a lazy few months in the field, this time with Night Cap. Welton Elan had been sold to America earlier in the year, not because he was in our bad books for kicking P (though we were certainly angry with him on that account) but because we have to sell a couple of horses each year in order to keep going. Although we enter all our horses (the novices included) under the name of my sponsors, the deal actually covers the expenses for only four of them.

We always have some youngsters around – and not simply because my mother is unable to resist buying anything that looks likely to make a top-class eventer. We also have to look to the future, when the older horses begin to fade. At the time of Burghley, we had eleven horses. There were the three advanced eventers (Priceless, Night Cap and Murphy Himself), four five-year-olds (Beneficial, Master Craftsman, Freeway and Bally McGinty), the two three-year-olds (Water Polo and Benevolent) and one two-year-old (Ben Hovis). Last, but by no means least, we had an amazingly youthful-looking 19-year-old chestnut called Dubonnet, who was still earning his keep by providing the working pupils with an ideal mount for their lessons.

Bally McGinty subsequently became the second horse we sold that year. Since we never buy any youngster unless we believe it has potential talent, there is rarely any problem in finding a buyer; word has gone round that we usually have a good horse for sale and people come to us. Having sold our normal quota of two, we still had ten horses to feed and were naturally delighted when Spillers came up with the offer of a deal that we couldn't refuse; they are now providing some of the food for our hungry eventers of all ages!

Murphy Himself was to compete in the new Audi three-day event to be staged at Chatsworth a month after Burghley. Thanks to his wonderful movement, he was joint leader with Mark Phillips on Distinctive at the end of the dressage but, whereas Mark went on to win, I had a fall across country at the Dog Kennels that was to confirm my long dislike of bounces. In this case there were three sets of rails involving two bounces; Murphy, who jumped in far more boldly than I had anticipated, found himself uncomfortably close to the second element and impossibly close to the third. He somehow managed to get over the final rails and stay on his feet; I almost succeeded in staying with him but eventually failed and landed straight on my head. Somewhat bewildered at finding himself on his own, Murphy then decided that the steeplechase area had been the most exciting part of the course, so he galloped back down the hill towards it. I still shiver when I think of the numerous ropes he jumped as he went flying off looking for action. He had paused and put his head down for a quick snack when a kind stranger managed to catch him – which, as I am all too well aware, can be a difficult feat.

As Murphy was being returned to me, Johnny McIrvine came hurtling across Chatsworth Park, looking like Barry Sheene on the moped that he had borrowed from his father-in-law, Roger Elliott. Having checked that I was all right, Johnny put me back in Murphy's saddle and the horse jumped the rest of the fences quite beautifully. Despite the fall, we were delighted with him. What a star, I thought, now he's proved he's got what it takes.

I had fairly severe headaches and felt rather groggy for three days after that fall, but was fine by the time I took Murphy to Castle Ashby the following weekend, hoping to finish the season on a better note. We had decided to try changing his bit from his normal gag to the much milder Dr Bristol and I very much regretted this decision when he took off with me around the cross-country course. He somehow managed to clear all the fences at this breakneck speed, but it was not an experience that I would care to repeat! I was still worried about ending the season on the wrong note when I took him to the Markfield Equestrian Centre in Leicestershire to give a lecture/demonstration. As luck would have it, there were some show jumping competitions there the following day; I decided to take part and the two bad memories were erased when Murphy won both the Newcomers and the Foxhunter.

By this time Hamish and I had fixed the date for our wedding. We had been thinking of waiting until after the 1986 World Championships in Australia, with the idea that we would then have time for all the preparations and for a honeymoon in some far away place. But the invitation for both of us to be on the British Airways team playing elephant polo in Nepal changed that plan. We decided to get married on 7 December and then fly on to Nepal for a honeymoon that promised to be somewhat different from usual!

This left us with little more than two months to prepare for the wedding and my poor mother had a hectic time. Hamish nobly offered to make his contribution to our efforts by repainting the white railings around the paddock, so that they would look smart for the reception that we were to have at home. We left him to start this laborious task while we were out for most of the day, and he was half way through it when we returned.

'Hamish,' we called to him, as we came back to view his handiwork, 'what *have* you done?'

He looked at us in some bewilderment. Poor Hamish happens to be colour blind and the tin of paint that he had assumed to be white looked, unfortunately, quite different to our eyes. We now had pretty pink railings around the paddock! They were, I hasten to add, repainted white before the big day.

The rest of our preparations went rather more smoothly. I was thrilled when the Duke of Beaufort, whom I had met in the days when he was still David Somerset, agreed that we could be married in Badminton Church. It has always been a very special place to me; apart from the early Sunday morning service that my mother, Dot and I attend when we are at home, I often pop into the church to say a prayer. We also have a high regard for the vicar, Tom Gibson, and his wife, Gloria.

The Duke later bestowed a great honour on me when he wrote and said that he would be delighted for me to wear the blue and buff colours of the Beaufort Foxhounds when I went hunting with them. It was totally unexpected; I decided that I would certainly avail myself of this special privilege by keeping at least one horse in for some hunting during the winter.

While the wedding plans were in full swing, I was preparing for a terrifying event at Wembley. This time there would be no horse to help me; I had been asked by my sponsors to give a twenty-minute talk during an insurance congress at the Wembley Conference Centre. They had been so good to me that I could hardly refuse. On many other occasions that year I had been rung to ask whether I could attend one of their functions. 'We'd love you to be there if you can possibly make it,' I'd be told over the telephone. If, as invariably happened, I had to decline because I was going to be at an event, I was given instant reassurance that they quite understood.

There was no such excuse to be made for this particular date on 13 November! The theme of the talk was to be 'The Pursuit of Excellence', with a special emphasis on how team-work can produce success in any sphere. There were some 1500 people present when I stepped up onto the rostrum and my voice had a definite quake in it for the first seven sentences. I was reading from the auto-cue, which transposed words onto a piece of glass in front of me, invisible to most of the audience, so it was assumed that I was being extraordinarily clever and delivering the whole talk from memory! I had been told that I must look up from time to time and glance to left and right across the conference hall, which I did in fear and dread of failing to find my place when I returned to the auto-cued words. By some miracle, I managed to get through without any awful gaffes.

The rest of the functions I attended towards the end of the year were rather more relaxed. Having been thrilled to win the annual awards given by *Horse and Hound* and the British Equestrian Writers' Association for the second year, I was staggered to learn that I had also been voted the Sportswriters' Association's Sportswoman of the Year. That took me on a return visit to the Wembley Conference Centre for a marvellous dinner when the Duchess of Kent presented the awards to me and Steve Cram (the SWA's Sportsman of the Year).

I also had my own 'hen party' to attend before the wedding. It took place in a London restaurant where Louise Bates and I met up with Lucinda Green, Lorna Clarke and Nicky McIrvine. Sadly, Lizzie Purbrick couldn't join us, because she was feeling the awful effects of injections administered all on the same day prior to a trip to Kenya. But a lovely bunch of flowers arrived from her husband, Reggie, with a note saying that she was in no condition to join the party.

The five of us were having a whale of a time, when a policeman arrived and came straight to our table. 'Is there a Miss Holgate here?' he asked. When I told him that he seemed to be looking for me, he went on to say, 'I'm sorry to inform you that this evening a BMW was seen to be driving at breakneck speed through Chippenham and we have reason to believe that you were involved.'

Louise and I had indeed been travelling rather fast since we were in danger of missing the train to London. 'I wasn't driving,' I said (like a true friend!). 'You'd better talk to Louise because it was her car.'

He insisted that he would still have to take me down to the police station to answer some questions, at which Lucinda became quite protective. 'You are *not* taking her out of here,' she said. 'Where is your badge? And where are your credentials?'

A heated argument followed at the end of which the policeman, plonking his helmet on my head, said, 'I can't fool you any longer,' before shedding some − but not quite all − of his garments. The whole thing had been set up by another absent friend, Kirsten Loyd!

FIFTEEN
Marriage

Never before have I packed so much into a single month. My wedding week began with a trip to Manchester to take part in television's *The Krypton Factor* together with three other sports personalities – Beryl Crockford (rowing), Jeff Thompson (karate) and Richard Ellison (cricket). When I saw the obstacles on the assault course they had prepared for the four of us, I had definite misgivings as to whether this was the right week to take on such a challenge! But I survived the ordeal without injury – though, it has to be said, with rather less energy in hand than Beryl. While I collapsed into a chair, she went off for a five-mile run.

Fear of injury was replaced by fear of making a complete fool of myself when we had to answer questions and when we attempted to display our 'mental agility'. To my utter amazement, I emerged as the overall winner and therefore had the marvellous opportunity of giving £5000 of Granada Television's money away. I had no time for any long considerations as to who the recipients should be, but I am still more than happy with my spur of the moment request that it should be divided equally between the Save the Children Fund and Riding for the Disabled.

The assault course for *The Krypton Factor* had been deep in mud, and so was our garden at Ivyleaze on the day before the wedding. I had collected my wedding dress in London that morning from Gina Fratinis (it had been my great good fortune to be introduced to her through Min Stevenson, who sells fabulous clothes at her shop, 'Image', in Bath) and the rain was descending as though from buckets as I drove home with Louise Bates. The newly erected marquee looked in danger of sinking in the relentless downpour.

My mother and Dot were working overtime as always. So was Mr Coombes, a local landscape contractor, who helped Mummy dig trenches around the marquee to stop water flooding in from the fields, before they laid a gravel path and lined it with fir trees. Louise was to

153

be in charge of our three page boys and two bridesmaids. In addition to the young 'Wols' (Harry and his sister 'P') there were Charlie Brownlow, Hugo Chance and Emily Moreton. If it were still raining in the morning, we had permission for Louise to take them through Badminton House and into the church by another route, which would save them from getting soaked.

Happily the Good Lord sent us a beautiful day. The sun was shining as Dicky and Paul from Capelli Hair Salon in London persuaded my unruly hair to look far more sophisticated than usual, and as Uncle Jack prepared to walk the bride down the aisle. But where on earth were our bridesmaids and pages? Wol – together with Gypsy Joe who was there to take our wedding photographs rather than solve the mystery of the missing children – raced off to Badminton House. In the anxiety of the moment, Louise had forgotten that she was only meant to go that way if it was raining; she and her group were discovered and brought in haste to join the blushing bride.

My cold fingers must have swollen as they warmed up again in Badminton Church and slipping the wedding ring on the bride's finger began to look like a silent comedy. Hamish tried and failed, so did I. Our families, facing towards us from the choir pews started to giggle, as did the little group at the altar. Hamish's best man, Johnny Gorman (who had organised a riotous stag party for him), did his best to force the ring on. Then our vicar, Tom Gibson, had a go. I'm not sure to whom I owe my thanks for the success of this joint venture, but the goal was finally achieved.

As I changed my name from Holgate to Leng, I thought of both my parents with tremendous affection and gratitude for a wonderful childhood and for all the loving support they gave as they taught me to cope with some of life's more difficult days. Mummy was looking fabulous in her new outfit, so were Dot and my new mother-in-law.

Hamish and I had a marvellous wedding day, with friends from around the world to join our celebrations and partake of the splendid lunch produced by Sarah Capper. Our local ladies – Mrs Fenton, the flower arranger, and Mrs Curnock, who made the vast and delicious cake – deserved gold medals. Our vet, Don Attenburrow, made a brilliant speech for the bride, as we knew he would.

Don entertained our many eventing friends by recalling an occasion when I was about 14 and he was studying the different tempo between canter and gallop. 'What difference do you feel between the two when you're riding?' he had asked me in all seriousness.

'Oh that's pretty obvious,' I told him, equally seriously. 'When you're cantering you feel you can stop, when you're galloping you know you can't.' This was not, as Don pointed out, a great deal of help to anyone studying the sequence of hoofbeats at canter and gallop!

Hamish gave a great speech and Johnny Gorman entertained us so well that everyone shouted for an encore as soon as he sat down. Johnny had been indirectly responsible for our honeymoon trip to Nepal by introducing Hamish and me to his sister, Rosanna, who is Publicity Officer for British Airways. This was swiftly followed by an invitation for the two of us to join David and Lucinda Green on the BA team for an elephant polo tournament in Nepal. Our chef d'équipe would be Concorde pilot Colin Morris, who flew out with his wife, Poppet, and also filled in as the fifth member of our team.

After one night in London, the newly-wed Lengs arrived bleary-eyed at Heathrow the following morning for the long and fabulous flight to Delhi, where we changed planes before travelling on to Katmandu. We then had a five-and-a-half-hour drive through magical Nepal to the jungle lodge called Tiger Tops, created by Jim Edwards and owned by him in partnership with a syndicate. Our rooms were built on stilts and we dined in a lovely circular building, with a log fire blazing in the centre. It seemed an unlikely place in which to meet Ringo Starr, Billy Connolly, Max Boyce and Barbara Bach (who played the Russian spy in *The Spy Who Loved Me*), but they were all there as members of the Cartier elephant polo team and therefore ready to do battle with us.

Lavenhams, who are used to clothing horses, had made splendid outsize rugs for the elephants. Harry Hall clothed our team of riders, which meant making outsize boots for Hamish. His feet are so large that I reckon he doesn't need a pair of skis when he takes a winter holiday on the snow and he was a truly amazing sight when kitted out for elephant polo. There were nine teams against us and, though Big Ham was one of our goal scorers, I'm afraid we didn't take British Airways into the semi-finals.

But we had tremendous fun, from the toss of the coin that decided which elephants our chosen team of four would ride in the first half before we swapped mounts, and selecting a polo stick of the right length. The sticks ranged from 90 to 130 inches and you waited until you were on board before taking your pick. Each elephant was controlled by a mahout, who sat behind its ears and gave mysterious elephant aids which seemed to be readily understood by these huge and obliging animals. The players sat behind the mahouts, strapped to the elephants' grey backs by surcingles that came over our thighs and allowed us to lean over for a swing at the ball without danger of losing our balance. David Green and I proved to be much more ruthless than our team-mates, who tended to make polite apologies when hooking our opponents' sticks or riding them off.

Since our polo ground was an airstrip, play was occasionally stopped while a plane came in to land. When anyone scored a goal, there were loud cheers from the many villagers who had come to watch the biggest and best tournament since elephant polo was added to the activities of Tiger Tops five years earlier. Greatly excited by the cheering, the elephants would add their own noisy trumpeting. We won our first match against the Scottish team and had our first thrilling view of a wild tiger the same night. But the following day we were put to shame by the Oberoi Ladies and, though we continued to enjoy a daily match, we were knocked out of the tournament. We are determined to get our act together if our chef d'équipe, Colin Morris, gives the same bunch of tearaways the chance to redeem themselves for British Airways.

As we couldn't win, the next best thing happened. The Tiger Tops Tuskers, representing the jungle lodge where we were enjoying such incredible hospitality, won a ferocious final between two local sides, defeating King Mahendra's team. Their victory was celebrated at a great party that night before we went our separate ways. Lucinda and David flew to Australia, Colin and Poppet returned home, while Hamish and I prepared for the second stage of our honeymoon. Organised by Nick Van Gruisen of ExplorAsia, it far surpassed our wildest expectations.

We began with a four-day trek in the fabulous Annapurna mountain range in the Himalayas. No less than eight people carried the equipment for just the two of us and we camped in a style that would have brought any boy scout's eyes out on stalks. Climbing the steep hills with our light rucksacks, we experienced a wonderful sense of peace in this isolated and incredibly beautiful country. Then, as our limbs grew weary after several hours' trekking, we would come to a little tented camp that our head Sherpa (Lakpur), our cook (Anna Cherring) and the six porters had gone ahead to prepare for us.

'Would you like hot water, boiling water, washing water, hot chocolate, hot milk, coffee, hot tea . . .?' Lakpur asked of a bemused Leng couple when we caught up with them on the first occasion. We spent three nights camping, always in a place with a spectacular view and our meals (served in the dining tent) would have done credit to a five-star hotel. Hamish and I didn't want it to end, even though ExplorAsia had more marvellous treats in store for us.

We spent Christmas Day near Mysore in Southern India, at the splendid Kabini River Lodge run by Col. John Wakefield, who took us on trips into the jungle to see leopards and in a coracle across the lake, to an island full of beautiful birds. After flying back north, we took a train ride to Agra to see the exquisite Taj Mahal; we saw in the New Year of 1986 drinking champagne, which Hamish had somehow managed to procure, in our lovely hotel room in Delhi. Returning home would have seemed a real anti-climax had it not been for the parties organised by our mothers and for the amazing presents that filled one room of the bungalow at Ivyleaze. We savoured the thrill of opening them by spreading it over three days.

After that we had to come down to earth. Hamish's nose was back to the grindstone once more as financial consultant and partner in the London-based J. L. Associates. This involves him in about three months overseas travel each year, while he looks after the financial affairs of British people working abroad. We have two homes – the bungalow at Ivyleaze and Hamish's flat in London – and we still don't manage to be in the same place at the same time as often as we would wish.

A new arrangement was worked out whereby Sue McMahon, a former Pat Manning pupil, comes to us each Thursday to school the horses, which leaves me free for a couple of nights in London, and that is a great help. Luckily for me, Hamish insists that he is happy to have a wife with interests outside the home; otherwise he feels that his long hours and frequent absences would be a source of friction.

It has worked well for me too, especially since delivering the essential message that I must have Big Ham around for support on the important eventing occasions when I need him most – not to mention the indomitable Hinge and Bracket!

SIXTEEN
Destination Australia

Both Hamish and I love ski-ing. Though we had made little impact on the mountain of work which had accumulated during our long honeymoon, we could not resist the invitation to join Sir Mark and Lady Norman at Klösters in Switzerland during the January of 1986. Hamish's mother came with us and she had a great time, having sensibly resisted our strenuous efforts to get her on skis.

Hamish looks rather like a giant spider on skis – all arms and legs. He is incredibly brave, as he proved on the day when we met the fearless Reggie and Lizzie Purbrick for lunch at the top of the cable car run on the highest mountain peak. The Purbricks were staying in St Moritz where Reggie, who will have a go at anything that is dangerous, had been invited to do the Cresta Run. He had survived several trips down the Cresta before keeping our lunch date on the top of a mountain, where he arrived looking like a true Brit – in corduroy trousers, shirt, tie and sweater.

The rest of us were muffled up to the nines and rather more suitably clad for the snowstorm that blew up outside while we were enjoying our boozy lunch. It was only then we discovered that the ski slopes below us were graded as a black run, the most difficult of all. Reggie had spent a grand total of 24 hours on skis; we wondered whether he could make it down in one piece.

'Point him downhill and let him run,' said Lizzie, whose own tremendously stylish way of ski-ing follows roughly the same rules.

Lizzie is the same on skis as she is on a horse: she goes flat out. As if the black run wasn't hazardous enough, she and Hamish deliberately ran into the back of each other. First Lizzie chased and caught Big Ham, then he picked himself up and went after her . . . and so it went on. We all somehow made it, Reggie included, without any broken bones.

Hamish and I flew home the next day to find Ivyleaze in the grip of a big freeze. My unflagging mother had, as always, done the early roadwork on the horses and I was due to take over, preparing Night

Cap for April's Whitbread Championships at Badminton and Priceless for May's World Championships at Gawler in South Australia. The frozen ground threw our training schedule out of the window. The first canter workout should have been on 7 February, but the canter field was like an ice-rink.

My mother searched for hills where we could take the horses – and found them. We adapted our training schedule, using the hill work to expand the horses' hearts and lungs in the same way that cantering would have done. We jumped in the indoor school at Badminton, where Brian Hyham somehow managed to squeeze us in. The place frequently resembled Piccadilly Circus, with Richard Meade doing dressage while Rodney Powell was cantering, some of the Duke of Beaufort's forty-odd hunters were trotting and I was trying to jump.

With the first event of the season (the Crookham Horse Trials at Tweseldown) only a few weeks away, finding somewhere to canter became crucial. Much to our relief, a local farmer, Richard Smith, came to our rescue. He had rolled and rotivated around the edge of one of his fields that had been ploughed before the freeze, cleverly making a dirt track on which to exercise his point-to-point horses. I owe him a huge debt of gratitude for allowing me to use it; no doubt Lucinda Green and other event riders, who also took their horses there, feel the same.

Lucinda and I, both due to compete in the World Championships in Australia, were more than happy to accept an indoor assignment during those frozen weeks. We had been asked to take part in a fashion show at Woburn Abbey, to be run in conjunction with a fund-raising dinner at which Princess Anne would be the guest of honour. The money would be split between the Save the Children Fund and the Horse Trials Support Group's Australia 1986 appeal, for which Rosemary Barlow worked non-stop. There would be three professional models joined by five event riders – David and Lucinda Green, Rodney Powell, Emma Wilkinson and myself.

That evening we drank liberal quantities of Piper champagne, trying to remember to get the level right so that we would look happy on the cat-walk – which seemed to stretch into infinity like the M5 – but wouldn't trip each other up or fall over the side! After our quick-change routines, as we were about to set forth in our smart outfits from 'Stephanie's' of Woburn, David Shilling was there to plonk marvellously exotic hats on the female heads. Happily, the event riders completed the course without any falls and a total of £20,000 was raised.

Outside the freezing weather continued, frustrating our plans by causing the cancellation of the Crookham Horse Trials. This was to leave the open intermediate at Aldon, near Yeovil, as my only chance for a competition with Priceless before he went into quarantine at Wylye in preparation for his trip to Australia. It proved to be an alarming experience. P was incredibly fit and the well-built Aldon fences were not big enough to make him back off and concentrate. Having jumped the first three quite well, he ran away with me – taking fences four, five and six at breakneck speed before I managed to anchor him. After that I didn't dare to let him out of a hand canter; I was too frightened of being carted again.

I was full of apprehension about the World Championships when Priceless went into quarantine, with Elaine to take care of him. By then two members of the chosen Australia squad had sadly dropped out. Lucinda, who had been due to defend her individual title, had been forced to withdraw because Regal Realm was lame. Mark Phillips had to be replaced (by Anne-Marie Taylor) when Distinctive contracted a contagious skin infection just before the quarantine began.

My own luck seemed to be holding out as long as I could solve P's braking problems. The next time I jumped him was over the schooling fences at Wylye, using a stronger bit, and I had him safely anchored. But I knew it wasn't the right time to start experimenting with new tack and I wanted him back in his usual Dr Bristol for the World Championships.

Bitting occupied a fair amount of my thinking that month. I had been riding Murphy Himself in a gag and, though there was nothing I could put my finger on, I wasn't happy with it. I kept banging on to Dot about wanting to change his bit. Knowing those moods of mine only too well, she realised that she would have to do something about it, if only to get a moment's peace. We took Murphy out to the steeplechase field and I jumped him repeatedly over a stone wall, each time with a different bit in his mouth.

'I like the scorrier best,' I told Dot, who was watching me with her experienced trainer's eye.

She agreed that Murphy looked good in this type of snaffle, which has four rings instead of the normal two. These increase the nutcracker action on the jaw, making it stronger than a plain snaffle. I put Murphy in the scorrier for his next event, a section of the advanced at Brockenhurst, and I shall never forget the magical ride he gave me over a wonderful cross-country course, as rain was sweeping across the lovely parkland. He used his brains, accepted control in his new bit and covered the ground swiftly with his long stride to win his section. Night Cap won the other advanced, giving my confidence a timely boost.

Fitting in the competitions and schooling the horses at home with almost daily trips to Wylye became a real test of stamina. The red Porsche clocked up more than 2,000 miles in four weeks and I spent nearly 2½ hours a day at the driving wheel, champing at the bit as I kept getting stuck behind slow lorries. True to form, Lady Hugh made sure that the regulations were strictly enforced for the British and German horses, plus the two Irish and Mark Todd's Charisma, who were in quarantine. On arrival at Wylye, I had to change my clothes and then go through a foot dip to get to the stables.

A mini-event had been organised by Lady Hugh for the horses in quarantine and, somewhat apprehensively, I decided this was the moment to put Priceless back in his familiar Dr Bristol bit. To my great relief, he gave me a really good ride across country and finished second to Charisma, despite a thoroughly sour performance in the dressage. The bad mood was because he regarded the whole thing as a total waste of time. As we plaited him up in the morning, he as good as said, 'If they think they can kid me that this is a proper one-day event, they can get lost.' He has never believed in wasted effort.

I think we were all feeling slightly fraught in the knowledge that the trip to Australia could be cancelled for any one of us if something went wrong. That fear became a reality for poor Andy Griffiths, whose great sense of fun had so enlivened the Wylye interlude. His Hullabaloo was unsound the morning after the mini-event and had to be withdrawn, reducing the Australia squad to six – Lorna Clarke, Ian Stark, Clissy Strachan, Mandy Orchard, Anne-Marie Taylor and myself.

Meanwhile Badminton was looming ever nearer. I stopped my daily trips to Wylye once the big event started, leaving Elaine to take Priceless for hacks while either my mother or Dot went to see him each day. I was therefore left free to concentrate on Night Cap and the cross-country course that Frank Weldon had designed for us. It seemed to me very technical; every line demanded a great deal of careful thought.

It was also incredibly wet. Both British National Life Assurance and Charles Follett's had taken hospitality marquees for the first time and I was pleased to visit them during the two days of dressage and shelter from the rain! As an already soggy Badminton Park was turned into a quagmire, there was much speculation as to whether the event would be cancelled before an announcement assured us all that the show would go on.

Night Cap, lying second after the dressage, was first to tackle the sodden cross-country course. He jumped a wonderful round, marred only by a run-out at the exit fence from The Lake for which I blame myself. When choosing a line that would take us across all three fences at a slight angle, I had failed to realise that Mr N might instinctively veer towards home if he floundered on landing in the water – which is exactly what happened. While I was leaning on his neck and in no position to help, he moved to the left and by-passed the exit fence for 20 penalties.

Despite that mistake, I was in fourth place at the end of the day, with Ian Stark a worthy leader on Sir Wattie. There had been rather too much drama and the Greens, who came to supper that evening, had suffered more than their fair share. David had lost a much-loved horse when Walkabout collapsed and died after the steeplechase; Lucinda, so often the star of Badminton, had twice parted company with Shannagh. We cheered ourselves up by watching, of all things, the video of the afternoon's cross-country. The reigning World Champion giggled as she watched the replay of her own mishaps, which included a lethal-looking high dive after Shannagh came to a sliding halt at the Stockholm fence. We laughed at my run-out with N – and felt much better for it.

Members of the public were not allowed to drive their cars into Badminton Park the following day. But they showed their true colours by trudging through the rain from their parked vehicles to watch the final show jumping and applaud Ian Stark's victory over Rachel Hunt, Rodney Powell and myself. As soon as it was over, Uncle Jack drove Dot to Stansted airport, where she was to take over from Elaine and look after Priceless on the marathon flight to Australia.

With refuelling stops at Winnipeg, Honolulu and Fiji, it took 33 hours from Stansted to Adelaide. Typically, during that long journey, Dot put P's welfare before her own – leaving her seat to check him every forty minutes or so, staying constantly aware of temperature changes so that she knew when to put rugs on or take them off, having no more than the odd cat-nap herself. She fed Priceless according to English time, avoiding any upset in his routine until he reached Australia. My mother and John Stone, Marketing Director of Spillers, had already made sure that there would be no drastic change in his diet once there by having samples of Australian fodder flown into England and analysed, with BNLA generously footing the bill.

Thanks to good air-conditioning on the plane and to stalls that were a good deal wider than those on the flight to Los Angeles – and thanks to the loving care shown by those in charge of them – the horses survived the journey to South Australia with the minimum amount of stress. Though muscle had wasted a little, Priceless looked bright-eyed and content when I rejoined him on Torrens Island, where the horses were completing their quarantine.

My mother had already flown out with Elaine, leaving Maita to deal with the post at Ivyleaze in our absence. It was shortly after my departure that she opened a letter addressed to me from 10 Downing Street. It read: 'The Prime Minister has submitted your name to Her Majesty the Queen for the Order of the British Empire . . .' I was asked to reply by return of post, saying whether I would accept an MBE.

Since I was on the other side of the world, Maita phoned Hamish at his office and read the letter out to him. After a stunned silence, he asked her: 'What on earth did Ginny do to deserve that?'

When Maita suggested that it might have something to do with Priceless, Ham retorted: 'Well I've ridden a horse and nobody's ever given *me* an MBE.'

I was equally stunned when Hamish phoned me in Australia to tell me the news. Needless to say, I was anxious for him to convey the message that I would be more than thrilled to accept an MBE. I only came down from cloud nine after his call when I suddenly thought: What happens if I make a mess of it in the World Championships?

SEVENTEEN
My priceless horse

It seemed slightly unreal as we drove across the causeway from the mainland of South Australia onto Torrens Island to realise that we still had four weeks before the championships began at Gawler. With just one horse to ride during that long stretch of time, it might be difficult to keep occupied and therefore all too easy to overdo the training. It was largely thanks to the wit and warmth of our marvellous liaison officer, Tim Dunn, that the days passed quickly and cheerfully for the teams from Britain, France, Germany and the United States, plus the two Irish girls and Mark Todd. Toddy's team-mates from New Zealand and all the Australian riders, whose horses were not subject to quarantine restrictions, had yet to arrive.

Various trips were organised – shopping in Adelaide, the cinema and theatre, a visit to see the Aussie animals in Cleland Park, which Lorna made memorable by riding a kangaroo. At the cinema, I inadvertently underlined the difference between male and female competitors by blubbering through *Out of Africa* while Ian and Toddy slept peacefully. Then, when it came to soaking up culture at the opening night of the Royal Shakespeare Company's brilliant production of *Richard III*, I regret to say that I was the one who dropped off to sleep in the second act!

We were all staying in curtainless, fairly basic accommodation at the Police Academy Fort Largs. The food was reminiscent of school dinners, so the Brits were delighted to go out for delicious suppers that were cooked by my mother and Dot at their rented house in Gawler. Since they had an eagle's-nest view over part of the World Championship cross-country course, we naturally spent a fair amount of time gazing out of the windows!

The training facilities on Torrens Island were much better than any of us had dared to expect, but I've no doubt the horses were pleased to have a change of scenery when they moved out of quarantine and into the stables at Roseworthy Agricultural College, which was to be their home until the championships were over. The British riders moved into a lovely rented house (where Lorna became chief cook, with Jenny Stark and myself as her assistants) until the students vacated their accommodation at Roseworthy College and all the teams moved there.

The horses' new-found freedom from quarantine coincided with a state of fretful indecision for some of their riders over whether or not to compete in the one-day event at Rynella. It was to be staged only nine days before the World Championship vetting and I wasn't sure whether I could afford to miss one of P's days of routine fitness work. I eventually opted to do only the dressage and show jumping. Judging from those who did the full test – among them Toddy (who won), Lorna and Anne-Marie – I may well have been wrong. The competition brought their horses on in fitness and gave the riders' morale a boost – except in the case of poor Mike Plumb, senior member of the United States team, who broke some ribs in a crashing fall. He was to prove his incredible courage by tackling all the fast routes at Gawler and finishing eighth, the best American placing.

The greatest stroke of luck for the Brits came when our chef d'équipe, Patrick Beresford, contacted his racehorse trainer friend, Colin Hayes, who invited us to use his facilities at the Lindsay Park Stud. Situated in the Barossa Valley, about 25 miles from Gawler, it is a really high-powered set-up and our eyes nearly popped out of their sockets when we saw the full circuit gallops, with a choice of all-weather surface or grass. The hospitality was fantastic. The horses were weighed and shod; their speeds were tested with electronic devices on the gallops and they were put out in separate paddocks to relax while their riders were taken out to unwind over wine-tasting or a pub lunch.

The competition was only a few days away when Hamish made his arrival, neatly timed to coincide with the parties! I collected him at Adelaide Airport, intending to change out of my jeans and into a smart skirt so that we could go direct to the Governor's party. The plan was fine, except that I had forgotten to put my skirt in the boot of the car.

'We'll go anyway,' said Hamish, settling himself into the back and leaving me to drive.

On arrival, I was told to drop 'the gentleman' at the main entrance and go round to the back of the house until the party was over. Jeans or not, I had no intention of playing chauffeur for the entire evening, so in I went to meet the Governor in my inappropriate attire.

'I'm terribly sorry for arriving without my skirt on,' I said to him, after a booming voice had announced Mrs Leng.

Seeing his startled look, I realised that wasn't quite right, so babbled on. 'I mean I know I've got trousers on – but, you see, I was picking up my husband . . .' At this stage, I swung round and made an expansive gesture with my arm to point out Hamish, who had been immediately behind me, only to find Clissy standing there. There are times when it would be better to keep your mouth shut!

I drove to another party, held on the evening before the vetting, with my jet-lagged navigator (Hamish) asleep on the map beside me. While wondering whether to wake him up, I suddenly spotted two car-loads of German riders speeding through Adelaide; all I had to do was follow them. This seemed fine until some traffic lights changed as we approached them. The two German cars stopped, but I did not. I hit the car at the back, which then hit the car in front. Germans spilled out of both vehicles to inspect the damage.

'Ah good,' they said, 'the lights still work so we go to the party.'

Prince Philip was there and he asked whether we were mixing much with the riders from other countries.

'Well Ginny has just been doing her best to get close to the German team,' said Hamish, before elaborating on my incompetence.

Our final week of training was marred by bad news. Two horses, one from New Zealand and another from Australia, dropped dead from heart failure, leaving everyone with the worrying thought that there was some sort of jinx over the whole event.

That particular fear faded as we inspected the course for the first time, but another took its place. For Phase A, the first section of roads and tracks, you went round the racecourse twice to the right. You then changed direction for Phase B, the steeplechase, and went round 1½ times to the left. Back to roads and tracks for Phase C, you did 1¼ circuits to the right before going off into the hills. How on earth was I to remember which circuit I was doing, how many flags I'd passed and which was the relevant kilometre marker while I was on this magic roundabout?

Phase D, the cross-country, was less confusing – but the ground was like concrete. Designed by Neil Ayers, who was also responsible for the Olympic cross-country, it was impressive until the long uphill climb after fence 12. The latter part of the course, from fence 13 to the final Wine Barrels at 32, was frankly disappointing. Apart from the Silo Bank and Rails (26 and 27) and the Gawler Gulley (31), those latter fences looked flimsy and rather insignificant. The terrain was largely responsible, since it would have been lethal to build spectacular fences on the steep uphill stretches, or on the sharp downhill gradient that followed.

Clissy agreed to go first for our team on Delphy Dazzle, only to learn that the draw had put her first in the entire competition. To her great credit, she maintained a cool and positive approach. At least she was in a happier position than America's Bruce Davidson, twice a winner of the individual world title, for whom we all felt so sad when his Dr Peaches was one of three horses to be failed at the first vetting. Clissy was to be followed in the team by Lorna on Myross and Ian on Oxford Blue. I was again given the chance of going last on Priceless, which was a great privilege.

Our two young riders, Anne-Marie on Justyn Thyme and Mandy on Venture Busby, competed as individuals and covered themselves in glory on the first day of dressage by finishing first and second respectively. Though back to third and fourth the following afternoon, they still did better tests than Britain's team members.

Priceless was feeling far from composed before the start of his dressage. He bucked as we moved from the early practice arena to the one we were to use before going in; he let fly again as we cantered towards the main arena for the start of our test. 'You little toad,' I thought, knowing that he had the whole thing sussed out and was well aware that all I could now do was sit and pray.

To my great relief, most of his trot work was excellent, but in canter he became more and more wound up until finally letting rip in the last movement down the centre of the arena, where he did at least four flying changes and about three bucks before we halted almost in the judges' laps. It was irritating to know that he could have done much better, but we were nevertheless lying sixth at the end of the dressage.

It had been raining incessantly that day and the rock-hard ground was topped with about two inches of soft and slippery mud when Dot and I went off early on cross-country morning to take a last look at some of the fences. Wood chips had been laid on selected take-offs and landings – but, if anything, they made the slithery topping even more treacherous.

I could see Delphy Dazzle slipping as I watched Clissy's round on the closed-circuit television at the stables. I also saw her fall in the water at Dead Man's Pass (fence 19), which was the one that worried me most. As far as I could see, she had done nothing wrong, so it looked as though our team policy to jump on the left route would have to be changed. I didn't have time to watch much more. With only 43 starters, I soon had to be aboard Priceless and away on that confusing magic roundabout.

Finvarra, the overnight dressage leader, was being tacked up while I was weighing out before the start of Phase A, and I was horrified to see him rear and fall over backwards. He seemed none the worse for this escapade, but it was an unhappy start to a day that went from bad to worse for poor Torrance Fleischmann and the rest of the Americans.

I had a good ride on the steeplechase, except when letting the excitement of the occasion go to my head at the second last fence. Seeing a long stride, I asked P to take off from far away and he slightly nose-dived as he landed, which certainly woke me up! My mind was occupied through most of Phase C thinking of how I was *not* going to take any similar risks across country.

Back in the Box for the ten-minute halt, Patrick Beresford thoughtfully left Lorna to pass on his instructions together with her own observations on the course, which she had jumped clear on Myross. First there was a quick resumé of the news so far. Clissy's fall and Lorna's clear had been followed by an unlucky slip-up between fences for Ian. Our two individuals had completed the course, Anne-Marie with a magnificent clear and Mandy with one refusal.

Lorna was brilliantly detailed as she ran through the course with me, mentioning each patch of slippery ground as well as every fence. I could choose my own route at the Jubilee JJ's (5 and 6), but was to remember that Ian had fallen going the long way. There were two changes of policy – I was to jump the water (9) on the far right and the Silo fences (26 and 27) the slow way. Unless P felt tired after the long climb, I could take the time-saving corners at 16 and 17. My final instruction was to go clear as quickly as I dared, without taking risks.

I set out with these words racing through my mind and almost fell off at the first fence, which was low and wide. Possibly blinded by the sun, Priceless seemed to misjudge the width and had to put his back feet down on top of the fence and then kick off again. He was livid and bucked twice before reaching fence 2 and settling into a rhythmic stride.

I still had to decide on my route at the Jubilee JJ's. Had I been riding as an individual, I would have attempted the direct route across two big parallels. But the team needed a clear round . . . perhaps I should go the long way . . . yes, I would take the same route as Ian. It may have been the wrong decision, since P almost slipped up at the very place where Oxford Blue had fallen, on the turn to fence 6.

Priceless was still full of running after the long climb; we took the two corners easily and sailed on downhill. We caught up with

Ireland's Georgia Stubington at the Silo and were stuck behind her for the next two fences. My shouts of 'Georgie, I'm behind you,' were drowned in the blare of the loudspeakers and she cantered along quite unaware of my presence until I found room to overtake. 'Georgie, I'm going by now,' I called, as I was almost beside her, and she instantly slowed down to let me pass.

It was a wonderful thrill to finish with a clear round and to find Hamish waiting in the Box to give me a big hug. There had been no less than 26 falls from 43 starters, but my incredible horse had once again carried me safely round. I had 17.6 time penalties and was lying second at the end of the day, as was the British team. New Zealand looked like gaining double gold, with their team out in front and Judith 'Tinks' Pottinger (who had jumped the fastest round across country) leading for the individual on Volunteer with 17 points in hand. I went with Tinks to the press conference that followed and it was a joyous occasion. She was so thrilled that you had to feel elated just to be with her.

Priceless seemed fine the next day. I took him out for a quiet walk before the vetting at Roseworthy College and saw Tinks, still looking happy, having a canter on Volunteer. There was no hint of the drama that was to come and once the British horses were passed (minus Mandy's Venture Busby, who was sore after losing two shoes on the cross-country and had been withdrawn) I didn't bother to wait for the rest of the vetting. I was looking at photographs when I was told that Volunteer had been spun because of an injured knee. At first I didn't believe it. When the message eventually sank home, I was totally devastated. I went in search of Tinks and we fell into each other's arms, both in floods of tears.

The whole picture had changed as our horses left for the show jumping at Gawler with our fabulous truck driver, Bruce Allison. Britain was now leading for team and individual gold, but the poor New Zealanders' expected glory had slipped away. Their only hope of a medal now rested with Trudy Boyce, who was lying second. I had been particularly pleased to see her do so well, because she was a popular part of our team at Ivyleaze a couple of years earlier when she spent six months with us as a working pupil.

'All right Trudy?' I asked, as we warmed up together for the show jumping.

'I think so,' she said, in a scared voice.

'Well, if it's any consolation, I feel just as sick as you.'

I was not kidding! Even though Trudy had one fence down, leaving

169

me with two in hand, the butterflies were still at work as I struggled with the familiar fear of starting before the bell or losing my way. Priceless had a much more positive attitude to the job in hand; he jumped out of his skin over the big course for a clear round. Britain had won the team gold comfortably from France and Australia, and I was the individual winner. Trudy had won the silver medal and Lorna the bronze, with Anne-Marie fifth – a remarkable achievement in her first championships.

As the individual gold was hung around my neck, I thought of that moment four years earlier when I had wondered how Lucinda felt after winning the world title. I felt fantastic, but I knew there would always be a little sadness in my memory of that day because the championship had been gained at the expense of Tinks's disappointment.

There was a marvellous party in the British Support Group's tent when it was all over. Our hosts – in particular the tireless Rosemary Barlow – had done so much hard work to raise the funds needed for us to compete in Australia; it was lovely to feel that we had made their efforts and their journey worthwhile. We were also happy for our chef d'équipe, for Henrietta Knight (Chairman of the Selection Committee) and for everyone else who had played a part in our victory. We were far from mouse-like during these celebrations, but we couldn't compete with the din in the next-door tent.

'We might as well join them,' we said, so we trooped next door to find the New Zealanders raving it up – with Tinks and Toddy (who had lost his chance of victory when Charisma fell in the water) at the forefront of their lively party. I am totally convinced that there can never have been a more sporting team competing in any contest, in any part of the world.

Looking back on those World Championships some months later I thought Priceless had done so much that, if any horse was to win after Volunteer's dismissal by the vets, he at least deserved it. He had jumped clear in the Olympics, in two European and two World Championships; he had proved worthy of his name.

By then Murphy Himself had won the French Three-Day Event at Le Touquet and the Remy Martin Trophy at Burghley; he was beginning to remind me of P with his quick thinking and well-developed sense of self-preservation, but he still had a great deal to prove. Priceless, at the age of 13, had done it all.

I kept wondering whether I should retire the older boy while he was still at the height of his glory. At first I thought I would leave the decision to Priceless. He has never been slow to let me know how he's feeling; he was bound to tell me when he wanted to call it a day. But then I started to tell myself that he was getting older, that he could not be expected to hold his own against younger horses at present-day standards. He was the reigning World, European and National Champion – so what more could he do?

Eventually, I decided to make the decision for him and his retirement was announced in October 1986, during the Horse of the Year Show at Wembley. P had always loved cross-country whereas dressage was never his favourite, so I would retire him to the hunting field where he could have fun doing the part he really enjoys. He showed his approval of this arrangement by giving me some wonderful days out with the Duke of Beaufort's foxhounds. He was a real gentleman, the best horse I've ever hunted.

By then we had arranged that I would keep him at home until after Christmas and then send him to Louise Bates. There are no prizes for guessing how she answered when I suggested that she might like to hunt Priceless with the Pytchley!

LUCINDA GREEN
Regal Realm

'There are very few extra special horses in the world, but we thought Regal Realm may be one of them.'

In 1971 a nondescript brown foal began his life in the wild terrain of the Australian outback. Eleven years later that same horse, transformed beyond all recognition, took on all comers to become the World Three-Day Event Champion.

This book is the enthralling account of that little brown stock horse whom Lucinda Green thought could be one of those 'extra special horses' when she bought him on impulse in 1980. And entwined in Regal Realm's story is that of her own romance and subsequent marriage to Australian event rider David Green.

Regal Realm's brilliant performance in the 1982 World Championships, his subsequent win at Badminton in 1983, team silver medals at the European Championships and Olympic Games in 1984 and team gold at the European Championships in 1985 will capture the imagination of horse lovers all over the world.

'A compulsively readable biography.'
Daily Telegraph

NORMAN THELWELL
Thelwell's Pony Cavalcade

'. . . while no horse could possibly look exactly like a Thelwell horse, all Thelwell horses manage to look exactly like horses.' Since Basil Boothroyd wrote those words in 1957, the term 'Thelwell pony' has passed into the English language. This collection of three of Thelwell's best-loved books, *Angels on Horseback*, *A Leg at Each Corner* and *Thelwell's Riding Academy*, is now available in paperback for the first time.

MICHAEL CLAYTON and JOHN KING
The Golden Thread: Foxhunting Today

'Foxhunting is the golden thread running through the history of the British countryside.' Lord Willoughby de Broke

In this book, Britain's foremost hunting correspondent – 'Foxford' of *Horse and Hound* – and John King, one of our best sporting artists, give a personalised view of every region and hunting country in the British Isles, from the incomparable turf of the Shires to the special character of hunting in Wales or Ireland. Every aspect of the sport is covered, from the organisation of the Hunt, hunting and breeding hounds, to suitable horses for different countries, the mysteries of scent, the habits of the fox, great modern hunting characters and the controversial issue of the threat to hunting from saboteurs and the Labour party. There is also an invaluable directory of Hunts and glossary of hunting terms.

Beautifully illustrated throughout with full-colour plates and numerous pencil sketches, this is a book for all hunting men and women, and for everyone who appreciates the beauty of the extraordinarily varied hunting fields with which we are blessed in the British Isles.

G. BOWERS
Hunting in Hard Times

Would that today's foxhunter enjoyed the 'hard' times so delightfully portrayed by the author as she describes her and her bachelor brother's hunting season in 'the unfashionable home counties' at the turn of the century.

The search for a suitable property, horses and domestic staff, dining with the neighbours, getting to the meet in those days before motorised horse boxes – and, of course, the ups and downs of the hunting field itself – are all amusingly shown in this charming evocation of a bygone age.

A facsimile of the original edition, illustrated with full-colour plates throughout, this book will delight all hunting people, horse-lovers and all those with a taste for old hunting prints.